Singing For Your Supper

SINGING FOR YOUR SUPPER

What They Don't Teach in School about an Opera Career

Dan Montez

Whole Note Publishing

Singing For Your Supper
What They Don't Teach in School about an Opera Career
By Dan Montez

This publication is designed to provide competent and reliable information regarding the subject matter covered. However, it is sold with the understanding that the author and publisher are not engaged in rendering legal, financial, or other professional advice. Readers assume all responsibility for their lives and decisions made as a result of reading or listening to (by audio version) the contents of this book. Laws and practices often vary from state to state and if legal or other expert assistance is required, the services of a professional should be sought. The author and publisher specifically disclaim any liability that is incurred from the use of application of the contents of this book.

Whole Note Publishing Edition
Copyright © 2008 by Dan Montez
All rights reserved.

Whole Note Publishing
service@danmontez.com
wholenote@optonline.net

ISBN print ed. 978-0-9801905-2-6

CONTENTS

Section II: The Business

Introduction

You will notice that there are a lot of disparaging comments about schools in this book. If you teach at or administrate at a school, try not to take this too personally. You are probably aware of the deficiencies of your program and are trying to do the best you can to teach your singers important skills. If you are a singer, you need to know that schools often have their hands tied regarding the amount they can teach you. This is because not all voice majors want to become opera singers. Most of the graduates at a school will not become opera singers for many reasons. Schools need to serve the majority. Schools need to teach classes that help the most people get what they want. They are businesses like any other money- making organization. Most singers do not have the personality and discipline it takes to be an opera singer--and it really takes a certain kind of personality.

However, for those that truly want to be opera singers, there are not many places they can go to get proper training. Even the conservatories don't usually teach business skills. Unfortunately, these conservatories and other institutions also do not even teach many important vocal techniques.

The book is divided into two sections that may seem to have

little to do with one another. But that's not entirely true. They work together to create a career. Education is not the goal of an opera singer, but only a tool that is part of his or her business. Both vocal techniques and business skills are missing from the curriculum of many vocal programs. This book is designed to fill in many of the gaps left by educational institutions for aspiring opera singers.

There is also another unique aspect of this book. It sometimes teaches concepts backwards. By backwards, this means that students sometimes need to begin with proper behaviors being spelled out to them. This may seem artificial to some, but proper and efficient vocal skills will not always evolve naturally.

Learning to act, sing or play tennis, for that matter, often require that you learn backwards. This is based on the belief that we don't always do things naturally. We all come with baggage and bad habits that have come to feel comfortable to us, but are not truly natural. As a result, sometimes the tennis teachers will have to teach their students how to hold the racket in the most efficient and natural way. This is faster than letting the student discover it for himself. Sometimes, singers need to have techniques of singing spelled out in a way that could potentially lead to very unnatural singing and a robotic adherence to various skills. But these skills are only meant to express how they would sing if they were doing so naturally. This is a danger, but it can also be a revelation. It depends if you intelligently use the information.

Acting is the same. Studying what people do when acting naturally can teach you a great deal about how you should look when you have a finished product. If followed too religiously, it can also look fake, pasted on, and inauthentic. But it is close. And speaking of doing things religiously, belief systems of all kinds often teach the same way. This is not an uncommon method for learning in the world. Many belief systems are based on handing out systems of behavior that are supposed to represent what individuals would do if they were good people. Certainly some belief systems are similar to the French School of voice training in that they prefer not to start with behaviors, but hope that good behavior will naturally flow from a good source. But they do not always. Most of us are pretty encumbered by bad habits of all kinds, many of which are a result of bad examples and bad environments. So having someone hand out a few ideas that would show us how we WOULD sing, act, or play tennis IF it were natural can be a great help.

We may start out artificially in our behaviors, but we ultimately need to make a leap and discover why these behaviors are and should be natural and efficient. If you take the techniques of this book and only learn them superficially, you will not do yourself any favors. Continually ask yourself, "Why is this better, efficient, or natural?" Remember, just because something feels natural doesn't mean it is. This is because habits can make things feel comfortable even when they are not.

Good vocal technique is part of your business. If you ever get to a point where you stop working on it, your business and career will suffer. In fact, they may end. Don't ever get to the point where you feel that you can't improve your understanding of vocal technique or your understanding of running your business. If you want to be an artist, you have to do some things that are not artistic. Get over that now and don't whine about it. Everyone has to learn how to deal with money and marketing, agents and auditions. It's not an easy world. But you can do hard things. If you picked up this book, you certainly already have a certain kind of personality bent on improving yourself. You'll be just fine.

Section One

The Voice

Chapter 1

A Word About Vocal Technique

I t's positively amazing how many schools and conservatory graduates go out into the world of professional opera to audition and haven't been taught many basic concepts in vocal technique. There seems to be a real disconnect between schools and the professional world. Most students find that, after eight years of advanced school training, they learn more in the first year of actually participating in the profession than they learned in all their time studying.

The purpose of this book is not to teach the basics of singing. But there are gaps in technique that are glaring, especially among singers trained in the United States. There are probably many reasons for this. One, for example, may be the domination of various nationalistic methods in certain schools.

John Miller's wonderful pedagogical treatise on this subject, *Techniques of Singing*, divides the playing field into four major camps: French, German, Italian, and English. In this book, he compares the methodology of these vocal schools to actual functional efficiency. In other words, he demonstrates what works and what doesn't work and which methods are based on physical facts.

Too many schools give great lip service to the Italian school of "bel canto." Unfortunately, these institutions easily brush aside the methods of the Italian school that don't serve their agendas. Most auditioning young singers fresh out of school appear to have been taught a mixture of French and German techniques.

The French school, for example, prefers to utterly deny the existence of vocal registration. The Germans, admit the existence of register breaks, but take great pains to hide, obscure, and minimize their effects. Americans also tend to ignore coloratura technique, which used to be a staple for all voice types, not just for "coloratura sopranos."

In discussing vocal technique, it is very important that one point be made: Every teacher has his or her own vocabulary. Teachers that seem to be contradicting one another may actually be saying the same thing. In that same vein, teachers can use the same word to mean absolutely opposing things. This is why it is so important for students of the voice to learn the vocabulary of the particular teacher with whom they are studying. It is also important that the student learn some of the different ways teachers teach.

For example, some teachers focus on hard work, some on relaxation. The "hard work" teachers accuse the "relaxation" teachers of creating wimpy voices with no power and no projection. The "relaxation" teachers accuse the "hard work" teachers of creating tension and ugly tone quality. Some teachers teach descriptively and visually. Some teach kinetically, trying to put people in touch with their bodies. Some teach intellectually, explaining all of the mechanisms of phonation, articulation, and resonation. Still others teach through demonstration, hoping that they connect with a student who has the talents of copying and mimicry.

This book certainly cannot be all things to all students of the voice. In fact, the book is limited by the lack of demonstration, and an inability to evaluate whether the reader is correctly implementing the techniques explained. So, learn what you can and find a teacher that doesn't avoid the issues discussed in this book. Teachers like this will be hard to find because many of them have been taught from generation to generation by others who have ignored some of these important things.

This book will ignite some controversy, especially among teachers who have ignored or are unable to teach these techniques. Watch out for school faculty members who will suddenly become defensive when confronted with these omissions. Unfortunately, it's not entirely the fault of the schools. Most of them are designed to teach students how to become teachers and not professionals. In addition, they need to serve students, the majority of whom have no real burning desire to pay the necessary price to become a seasoned professional.

Too many students these days have little desire to learn anything outside the demanded curriculum. They will jump through all the hoops extended by their professors, but seem to have little interest in creating their own hoops.

Your success in becoming a professional classical singer will be based less on your innate talent and natural singing voice than it will be on your personality, tenacity, desire, and hard work. I spoke about these necessary personality traits in my last book, *Don't Believe It! How to follow your dreams in spite of those who say you can't*, so I won't rehash those things here. However, if you never lose your desire to improve your technique and learn to love the practice more than you love the performance, then you can make it. The majority of your life will be spent rehearsing and not performing, and if you hate it, you'll burn out in no time. So let's get to work.

Chapter 2

Legato and Vibrato Technique

Since this book is not about basic vocal technique, it will not begin with discussions of breathing and support. However, some elements of breath management will be discussed in a later chapter. Basic breath management is something you should understand by the time you begin studying the things in this book.

Perhaps one of the most misunderstood techniques of singing is basic legato technique. Again, schools give lip service to this idea, but they are also responsible in large part for actually destroying all clarity and understanding about this issue. Why? In part, this is because most school administrations are more attached and beholden to their choral programs than their opera programs. And this brings up an interesting starting point for a discussion on true legato singing:

Is there a difference between vocal technique used in a choir and vocal technique used in opera singing?

If you ask this question of most choral conductors, they will generally say that there is little or no difference. At least, that is what they want to believe. If they say this, they are wrong--especially if they subscribe to English school choral ideals rather than those of the Italian school.

A classical vocal training is all about efficiency. English choral technique, although producing a beautiful product, is not natural to the voice. Those who teach this choral technique are concerned with unity of tone. "Sound like your neighbor" is the mantra of most American choral conductors determined to "blend" the voices into one another. However, the human voice, naturally produced, is completely unique. No one singer should sound like any other singer. This is why a classically trained voice will often stand out in a choir, especially a choir filled with untrained voices.

Italian opera choruses, on the other hand, are filled mostly with trained singers, all encouraged to sing with their own unique sounds. Do they stand out? Well, one could say that they equally stand out, creating a fuller, more colorful sound than mostly anemic English choirs. So, when a classically training singers are required to sing in a college choir as part of the school's curriculum, they are often subsequently forced to manipulate various areas of their voice to conform to the sound of the whole. This is worse than unhealthy for those desiring a solo career.

Many vocal professors are also in charge of the choral program in their schools. Therefore, as they teach classical principles to their private students, they often undermine those students with their choral ideals.

That being said, blending isn't the worst problem with the schools. There are two other basic techniques of a classical training that are generally treated as enemies to good choral technique. These are legato technique and vibrato technique. Choral conductors will usually admit to the second, but deny that the first is a problem. In fact, many conductors will claim that they insist on producing a smooth, even legato, but actually have no idea what they are talking about.

This may all seem rather harsh, but classical singers who have any intention of becoming opera singers need a wake-up call. The problem has become widespread and therefore merits a more in-depth discussion of the human voice and how it works.

The Foundations of Legato Technique

The human voice is not a piano. It is not a guitar or a clarinet. It has no frets, keys or buttons to assure pitch. As a result, we shouldn't use our voices as if they are made this way. It is best to envision the vocal cords as similar to a rubber band. Have you ever stretched a rubber band and plucked it? The more you stretch it, the higher the pitch goes. Violin strings do the same thing. The tighter they get, the higher the pitch. There are muscles attached to your vocal cords that elongate and shorten the cords to create different pitches. Now, there are only two ways for a person to get from one pitch to another pitch:

1. Open the vocal cords and sing the first pitch. Close the vocal cords. Stretch the cords to the new pitch. Reopen the vocal cords and sing the new pitch.

2. Open the vocal cords and sing the first pitch. While you continue to sing and keep the cords open, stretch the cords to the new pitch.

Now, which way is the most natural and efficient way to sing? Every time you have to close and reopen the vocal cords, you are creating a certain degree of vocal fatigue. When you do it over and over again between every note, you are doing something not only unnatural to your voice, but something detrimental to a healthy voice. You will also sabotage your ability to sing for extended periods of time without vocal decay.

Now, another question: If singers use method two in moving from one pitch to another, what will they hear? Answer: all of the notes in-between. This is a revelation for most choral teachers. In fact, too many of them give contradictory instructions like, "Connect one note directly to the next note, but don't sing any of the pitches in between." You cannot do both. If you are connecting one note to the next, your cords will remain open and you will hear the in-between notes. Period. If you don't sing those in-between notes, you must close your cords between the notes and are therefore not connecting.

As choral conductors obsess about the obliteration of sliding, scooping, crooning, portamento and other connective techniques, they are destroying line, legato, connection and the true power of the human voice to phrase like no other instrument can.

Ironically, instruments, especially over the past one hundred years, have increasingly attempted to imitate the natural human voice. The violinist, for example, waggles the left hand to imitate the human vibrato. The more advanced a string player gets, the more they slide their fingers up the string to move from one pitch to the next in the middle of a phrase. Woodwinds regularly pulse their breath to create an artificial vibrato as well.

Interestingly enough, choirs spend most of their time trying to sound like instruments, jumping from one straight-toned pitch to the next. If choirs just admitted that this is what they were doing, it would be fine. The purpose of these attacks of choral singing is not to diminish the beauty of what they can create. They can do much what a pianist can, which is actually quite a lot.

But the solo voice can do so much more.

Portamento and In-between Notes

In singing in-between notes, it is important not to be embarrassed about them. What this means is that your in-between notes need to be just as loud and vibrant as the note you are both coming from and going to. Is this clear? Singers, who are beginning to understand the need to sing these in-between notes in order to have a legato sound, often begin by singing them weakly or by backing away from them almost as if they are embarrassed to sing notes that are not directly written in the score. Don't be embarrassed! In fact, when you are learning, practice by starting on one pitch and, as you leave the pitch, keep all the volume, power and vibrato you can muster. Sing those intermediate notes proudly!

There are two basic ways to sing in-between notes. One is with vibrato and the other without. "Crooning" (like that of Bing Crosby) is the one without vibrato. "Portamento" is the kind with vibrato. The word portamento is not simply a specific technique used when indicated by a composer. It is one of the most misused and misunderstood words in schools today.

Portamento comes in different flavors. But those flavors all have one thing in common: they are all nothing less than connected notes. This is one of the great secrets of professional opera singing. It is also one of the most misunderstood ideas in voice teaching today. Portamento IS the foundation of all legato singing required in most opera. Accept that definition before moving on. Portamento is necessary to shape a phrase, sing over an orchestra, and take the pressure off of the vocal cords.

Portamento means that you sing the in-between notes with a vibrato. The vibrato is uninterrupted from the moment of the originating note until the end of the pitch of destination. Here is a picture of the difference between a croon and a portamento.

Now, as for the different flavors, one can sing a strong, emphasized portamento, or a quick, lighter portamento. A portamento used in Puccini and Verdi will be different that that used in Mozart. But here is the important thing to understand: It is always there! It doesn't matter if you are singing Monteverdi or Wagner, connection is connection and legato is legato. The in-between notes must be there even if they are so rapidly sung that they are nearly imperceptible.

The biggest roadblock to learning to sing a correct portamento is that most singers today have little control over their vibratos. For example, amateur singers who have developed a basic vibrato may be completely lost when they first try to maintain a vibrato while leaving a pitch. If you have never done this, begin by trying to sing a vibrato on any note. Once it is going, try to go flat--out of tune, if you wish. See if you can keep the vibrato going as you do this. For many, it's not so easy. When most singers try to sing the in-between notes for the first time, they sing a vibrato on the first note and the second note, but straight-tone while traveling from one to the other. However, the goal is to keep it going during the entire phrase through all of the in-between notes!

Another roadblock to doing this is that if you study the picture above comparing the croon to a portamento, you will notice that in the case of the portamento, the quickest way between note A and note B is not a straight line. This goes against our intuition. When we leave a note, we want to go directly to the next note. However, the vibrato is a fluctuation in pitch. This means that, if it is going, you will sometime actually be moving AWAY from the subsequent pitch and not toward it. It is sort of two steps forward, one step back. In allowing for a vibrato, you must allow a fluctuation of pitch to occur while traveling. One might compare this sound to the imitation of a ghost:

Before you go on to the next technique, master the previous one first. Once you have the vibrato under control as you leave one pitch and approach another, you will be ready for the next rule of the portamento.

Rule of the Highest Note

When applying portamento to all notes that you wish to connect in a song, another problem arises. Which vowel does one travel on? If there are two notes, and each note has a different vowel assigned to it, which vowel belongs to those in-between notes? The general answer is: the vowel that belongs to the higher of the two notes. Here are two examples:

You will notice in the example above that the first set of pitches requires an ascending portamento. This means, that in general, you will travel on the vowel you are going to and not the vowel you are coming from. This will require you to put the consonant belonging to the higher pitch (in this case, the "D" of dog) down on the previous or lower pitch. In the second group of pitches, you will travel on the vowel you are coming from and put the final consonants on the lower note (the "RGE" of large will be connected to the front of dog). Now, look at the next example:

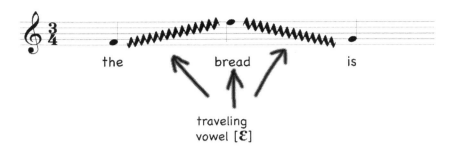

In this case, notice that the highest note of these three pitches is in the middle. As a result, you will use the vowel associated with the highest note to both ascend AND descend to and from the center pitch. Here is an example of a longer passage of music and how you would analyze it for in-between notes:

The diagonal lines above illustrate which vowels should be sung on the in-between notes. Notice that the [ɑ] vowel of "grembiale" is the vowel of choice when moving both up to the "C" and down away from it. Notice the same thing on the [o] of "mandero."

Now, remember as you sing these that your goal is to not only sing the portamentos on the appropriate vowels, but to retain your vibrato at all times while you are doing it. This may take some practice.

Are there any exceptions to the Rule of the Highest Note? Yes, and this is where some of the confusion starts regarding the word portamento. From time to time, composers will want a portamento to ascend from the vowel of the first and lower pitch. When they do this, they will generally do one of two things. The first thing they will do is write a portamento mark, which looks exactly like a slur mark--but it is not a slur mark. The second thing they may do is write the word "portamento" or simply "port." for short. In addition to the one at the beginning of the previous example, here is another popular example of the portamento mark:

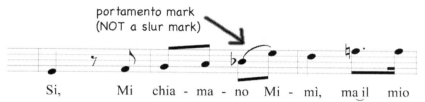

In this example, the voice will use the vowel associated with the lowest note and portamento up, putting the final consonant of that note on the upper pitch. This is less common, but it happens and you need to keep your eyes open for this. As for the rule applying to descending, this never happens. You will not find any composer who wants you to descend on a vowel not belonging to the highest note. The exception only applies to ascending, not descending.

Different Kinds of Portamento

As discussed previously, there are different flavors of portamento. The differences are usually achieved by changing the weight of the in-between notes. There are two kinds of lighter portamento. A lighter portamento maintains the same basic pressure on the in-between notes that is on the originating pitch and the goal pitch. One type of lighter portamento is one that is used rapidly and the other type is used more slowly. The faster one attempts to completely draw more attention to the destination pitches than the legato connection. It is used primarily in Baroque music and some Classical music. The other one is used mostly in Classical music and art songs. Intensity of tone and support doesn't change or waver while traveling from one pitch to the next.

Another type of portamento is one where the in-between notes are slightly weighted. More time is taken on the notes so as to draw some attention to this connection. This medium type of portamento is often used to prepare for cadences or phrasal climaxes in Classical repertoire. It used more constantly in Verdi and Puccini operas.

Heavy portamento is that which heavily emphasizes the in-between notes to the point that they become more important than the originating and destination pitches. This is used in medium to heavier repertoire mostly from the Romantic Period and beyond. It is used mostly for dramatic emphasis and not necessarily for technical reasons. However, there is an argument to be made that it can technically assist a singer in less lyrical passages with large jumps between pitches.

Straight Talk on the Vibrato

If you want to compete in the world of opera, you need to have some basic control over your vibrato. One of the biggest misconceptions about the vibrato is that you are stuck with the one you have. Vibrato speed is absolutely controllable. There are too many singers getting out of college today that have a vibrato that is too fast (bleats) or too slow (wobbles) or is too harsh (amplitude to large) or too insubstantial (amplitude too small).

There is a natural speed to vibrato that is generally between six and seven oscillations per second. They word "natural" here means that it is the relaxed, efficient, and takes the most pressure off of the vocal cords. Just like it took tenors years to figure out how to hit the first "high C," it took singers many years to figure out the natural and most efficient speed of a vibrato. Serious discussions about vibrato control are fairly recent. Even singers from the early twentieth century hadn't completely figured it out. Many of the stars of the so-called "golden age" of singing couldn't handle their support and vibrato the way many modern singers can. We have come a long way, even in the past fifty years.

Learning to control vibrato speed and get rid of bad bleats and wobbles in no easy task. It will take many hours in the practice room studying how the vibrato works in relationship to breath management.

16

But here are some ideas that may help. In general, vibrato speed is impaired when the diaphragm (the inhaling muscle) and the abdominals (responsible for exhalation) are not balanced. When support is higher, closer to the rib rim, or "tucked" the vibrato tends to speed up. When support is too low in the abdomen, it slows down.

Support pressure must adjust as pitch adjusts. Higher notes require more support and lower notes less. Unfortunately for students who never learned to differentiate between the two sets of breathing muscles and were told (especially in choirs) to just "tighten their tummies," the abdominals usually dominate. Why? Because they are generally many times stronger than the diaphragm. When this domination occurs, the support (active resistance between BOTH sets of muscle groups) moves upward and the vibrato speeds up.

This is why many beginning singers, who still have weak diaphragms, also begin with faster vibratos. In fact, one can audibly recognize amateur singers during an audition when their vibratos speed up while making jumps to higher pitches. Their inclination is to want to "add support" in order to hit the higher notes. However, their diaphragms are not usually up to the task of resisting their abdominals and so the entire support mechanism tucks in and their vibratos begin to bleat.

In order to maintain "sameness" in vibrato speed between pitches, adjustments have to be made in the support mechanism. Generally, more diaphragm engagement is required. Because the diaphragm is the inhaling muscle, many describe increased support as a feeling of inhalation or expansion during phonation. As the diaphragm increases its work while the pitch rises, the vibrato can maintain a constant speed.

There are times during a song that a professional singer will use the vibrato as a tool to increase excitement in the phrase. One example is in ending most Verdi arias. Traditionally (which means it is not always in the score), the final note of a Verdi aria (especially a bel canto aria) will be held as the accompaniment continues with its um-pah-pah in the last couple of measures. The voice cuts off with the accompaniment, but right before that cut-off, the voice will often abruptly speed up the vibrato. Here is a graphic of what is often written verses what is traditionally done in performance:

What's Written

de - lizia al cor!

What's Done

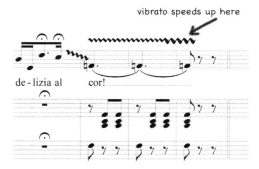

vibrato speeds up here

de - lizia al cor!

Another time a student may use vibrato control is on certain chromatic pitches in a song. For example, Mozart arias frequently use appoggiaturas as follows:

stun - den   mei - nem   Her - zen   mehr   zu

In this example, the note marked with an asterisk can be effective as a straight tone. The reason for this is that because the vibrato is a fluctuation in pitch, and the pitch in question doesn't fall into the normal harmony or key of the song, the audience might question whether or not the note is an accident or whether or not the singer is singing out of tune. Straight-toning notes that are unusual, unexpected, or don't fit into the key is a common technique used by singers. It can take doubt away from the audience and draw even greater attention to the fact that the note purposefully doesn't fit the normal harmony. An ability to turn the vibrato on and off at will is a necessity to execute this kind of technique.

Teachers are often afraid to tell their students that they have problems with their vibratos for fear that their student will begin to manipulate their voice and cause unnatural sounds and tension. This stems from the fears of the French school in particular. It is a phobia against drawing attention to the mechanics of singing. This obsession with singing "naturally" often becomes an impediment to singing naturally. Students always deserve to hear the truth about all of their problems. Students rarely come to a teacher doing everything correctly and naturally. Most students come with unnatural habits that feel natural to them because they are habits and have to be undone. Sometimes manipulative techniques MUST be employed to break them of these habits before the student is taught to embrace the most efficient and natural methods of singing. Intelligence is required on the part of the teacher and student.

Final Thoughts on Legato and Vibrato

Connecting the notes of a phrase with a supported portamento and utilizing a natural vibrato are two of the hardest things a singer can learn to do correctly. However, they are vital to a stage career. Far too many students are leaving the university or conservatory without any control over either one of these. Educational institutions are often intellectual, yet not always practical. The opera world is full of traditions that must be studied. One can argue forcefully that we need to perform according to the composer's "intentions," but if that doesn't get you a job, you are in trouble. You should study and try to determine the composer's intentions, but your knowledge needs to be coupled with an awareness of the traditions as well.

In addition, educational institutions would do well to separate their choral and opera disciplines and admit to their disparate goals and objectives. As a student of the voice, you should emulate, model, and even imitate the technique of professional opera singers. Don't imitate the tone; you have your own. Imitate the technique. In order to do this, you must listen regularly to professionals and dissect what they are doing. Listen in particular to their in-between notes, how they travel from one pitch to another, the vowels they use and how they use their vibratos.

Are there exceptions to any of these ideas? Of course, there always are. There are times you don't want any legato in your singing and there are times you need to take out your vibrato. However, breaking the rules is a right given to those who have learned to keep the rules. The spirit of the law often manifests itself after learning the letter of the law.

If you are being taught or coached by any one in denial of the importance of legato technique or by someone afraid to discuss the vibrato as expressed here, get a new teacher. Certainly this is difficult and maybe drastic advice, but your teacher is your servant and not the other way around. If he or she stops serving your interests in having a career, then you need to move on. If, after reading this book, you feel it doesn't speak to your interests, then throw it away and move on. But before you do, test these things intelligently and see if they make sense and if they help you achieve the kind of career you want.

Chapter 3

Coloratura Technique

T here was a day that everyone had to learn coloratura technique. Vocal flexibility should be required for all voice types. There is a false idea that has been floating around for many years now that heavy or dramatic voices just can't move quickly and just can't be flexible. Nothing could be further from the truth. The truth is that certain voice types are no longer trained in coloratura technique. Today when opera houses want to do *Macbeth* or *Nabucco*, or a serious Rossini role like those in *Tancredi* or *Semiramide*, they are limited in who they can choose to cast because singers aren't properly trained. It was wonderful to see Samuel Ramey's big voice easily circumnavigate the coloratura in *Semiramide* in recent years. Thanks to singers like Marilyn Horne and others, more and more teachers are reintroducing this technique in the United States. Unfortunately, not enough teachers have any idea how to teach this technique and we are often left with the blind leading the blind from generation to generation.

Coloratura technique is an issue of flexibility and not strength. When many trained, powerful singers try it for the first time, they feel uncoordinated. This is normal. Developing this technique takes time and can't be learned over night.

When many college teachers hear it for the first time, they disparage the sound. This is because too many teachers have their minds set in the acoustics of the small practice rooms and studios at colleges and don't realize that sounds have to be exaggerated for the big stage. Many choral directors, interestingly enough, understand this concept with the subject of diction. They understand that you exaggerate your diction at times so that the words sound normal in a large concert hall or cathedral. Coloratura technique requires the same adjustments depending on the room in which you are singing. In close proximity, the sound can sound like a "machine gun" technique, not always pleasing to the ears of teachers.

Marilyn Horne has often been criticized in universities for this reason, and yet teachers need to compare her recorded broadcasts to her live performances. Live, one can clearly see how this technique does its job. Today, Jennifer Larmore has taken over much of Horne's repertory and is another fabulous ambassador for this technique. Her recordings show off the clarity of her melismas, but unfortunately, sometimes they show the exaggerated nature of coloratura technique that simply doesn't appear on stage. On stage, she sounds clean, clear, and precise. When teachers teach, they need to take into account the room for which the singer is being prepared. This doesn't just apply to coloratura technique, but also to projection in general. Too many teachers (and conductors for that matter) apply small room projection ideals to the big stage, artificially darkening the voice, or taking out necessary resonators that are foundational to an opera career.

There should be a relationship between projection, having a real body connection to the sound, and the methods used to produce coloratura technique. There are some opera singers out there who are obsessed with speed to the point that they have lost their body connection and attempt to do their melisma technique in their throats. Some are actually fairly skilled at this and get the voice moving about as fast as Woody Woodpecker. Unfortunately, they often sound like Woody Woodpecker in the process. They lost their connection to their body and have great difficulty projecting their quickly moving voices past the second row in a legitimate opera house. This just adds to the notion that coloratura singers must have light, insubstantial voices. This simply doesn't have to be.

The Technique

Coloratura technique is best demonstrated rather than described. The description may sound bizarre and some will be left scratching their heads. As an added help, a website address will accompany each example where you can listen to an example of the described sound.

The first rule of coloratura technique is to throw your pitch out the window. As you learn the technique, pitch will return to the extent it is supposed to return. However, in order to create precise pitch, one has to first lose pitch. Keep in mind, at least while you are learning, that the technique is more important than the pitch. Say it over and over to yourself. If you go for the pitch first, you will often ruin the technique and it simply won't work.

Before jumping in, it important to explain some of the reasoning behind the technique. The technique, in part, exists to compensate for pitch issues created by the natural vibrato in the voice. Remember, a natural vibrato oscillates at six or seven oscillations per second. This oscillation is a fluctuation in pitch. Now, if you are singing a scale with your vibrato in tow, you will be fine as long as your tempo is slow. But what happens when your tempo begins to increase? If the vibrato is still present, it will start to get tangled up with the intended pitch of the song. You will be on the upper pitch end of your vibrato on one note and the lower end of the vibrato on the next note. This will make you sound out of tune and feel that you will either have to abandon your vibrato (creating subsequent tension and a lack of line and portamento), or you will struggle to sing the pitch on the page in spite of your vibrato and crash and burn. Coloratura technique exists to solve this problem. It temporarily brings your voice onto the pitch at the same tempo of the music. It accomplishes this by use of a pulsing technique without the need to stop the vibrato.

In order to learn the technique, you first need to slightly disassemble your voice. Begin by singing a pitch without your vibrato. (If you can't control your vibrato or have difficulty starting and stopping it, you will have difficulty with this technique. Learn that first.) Now, while you are holding the pitch, see if you can pulse your stomach, subsequently pushing your straight tone off of the pitch. Here is a diagram of Example 1:

Audio examples can be heard at the following web address:

http://wholenotepublishing.com/audio/examples.html

Now, once you have copied this sound, try to do it with a metronome. Slowly learn to speed it up to an even pulse. You may feel uncoordinated at first, or you may get it right away. Once you do, you can go on (Listen to Example 2 online):

It is important to note here that this technique should not be breathy and that your support should be unimpaired. As an analogy, imagine a balloon that has been tied off so no air is escaping. Now poke the balloon at any tempo you wish. You notice that even though you are poking, no air is escaping because it is tied off. This is similar to what we want with coloratura technique. Your support should be separate from this skill. You continue to hold back your air, but you pulse at it. You do NOT pulse the actual air. This is important.

Many make this mistake without a teacher present to correct them and change air pressure during the technique. The tone needs to remain pure.

You will notice that when you pulse in this way, it will throw you off pitch. In order to do coloratura technique, however, the pitch that you want to establish in your music is not at the bottom of the pitch, but it will be at the top of the pitch change. As you fluctuate the pitch, the higher pitch is the one that is in your music and you are coming from underneath the pitch. Once you think you understand this, and you can control the speed of your pulses, attempt to do the following exercise up the chromatic scale (Example 3):

You will notice that the pitch goes up to the note from underneath every time the abdominal muscles are pulsed. Try to master each example before you go onto the next one. They will get progressively harder and build upon the previous example. You will notice that in the previous example, that in the five notes of each pitch the first and the fifth were somewhat accented more in spite of the fact that all five are pulsed. This is because most melismas reflect normal sixteenth note groupings of four notes to a beat. It is good to get into a habit of being able to slightly accent the actual beats of a song containing melismas when rehearsing them slowly. They won't stand out in this way at full speed but simply clean things up. Once you have mastered example three at various speeds, it will be time to begin changing pitches while you pulse.

Before you put your vibrato back in, try the technique without it. Here is an example of a five-note major scale up and down with the technique rendered slowly (example 4--no vibrato):

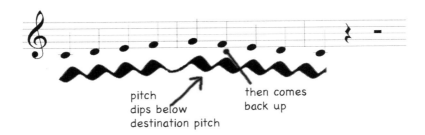

Remember, you will never sing this way at the speed of the previous example. But this is how you would practice slowly to set up a foundation for a faster tempo. You will notice that the scale can be disconcerting and create some pitch confusion. You will also notice that the pulses are different on the way up as they are on the way down. (Listen to audio example 5 with vibrato).

You will notice that at the top, coming down, for example, you will have to dip below the pitch you want to go to and then come back up to it. This kind of coordination at break-neck speed is difficult. Don't feel badly if you don't get it right away. The pitch change is minimized at higher speeds. (Listen to audio example 6).

You should notice with this last example that the first pitch must start almost underneath as well in order for the pulse to catapult the voice up to the correct pitch and begin the coloratura process. This becomes even more necessary when moving from a legato technique to a coloratura technique without a breath. Here is an exercise that you should master before going on (demonstrated in three repetitions in Example 7...but you should continue up the scale further):

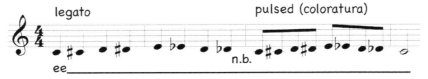

In this last example you will notice that the vibrato is clearly present during the slow section and on the final note. In addition, you should notice that the coloratura section has a vibrato quality--this means that one can tell that if one were to stop on ANY note of the coloratura section, that the vibrato would be automatically present. This is important to understand. When you first start learning this technique, you may feel the need to "pulse while straight-toning" during the coloratura sections. But ultimately, the goal is to have the pulse temporarily interrupt the vibrato's natural pitch fluctuation. This means that when a pulse isn't present, the vibrato remains present in its natural state. Now try the exercise above with a major scale rather than a chromatic scale. This time, also add a vowel change in the middle of the sequence (Example 8):

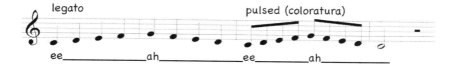

You should master the above two examples moving up the scale to the top of the passaggio (not far beyond). It is vital that while you do these exercises, you do not do them in the throat, but with the body. Speed and coordination with the body will take much time for most singers. Be patient and don't create shortcuts to speed by singing in the throat or disconnecting from the core of your sound. Keep it slower until you can speed up. Fast speeds can come as you lighten the technique.

You should be able to sing coloratura at any normal speed. Often, people that learn it incorrectly find that they are one trick ponies. They often can only do coloratura at exactly twice the speed of their vibrato speed! This is because they aren't really fighting the vibrato but going along with it. Unfortunately, when they switch from coloratura to legato technique their vibratos bleat away on a single pitch sounding as if they are still doing coloratura technique.

Correctly executed coloratura technique can be produced at any speed because the technique is not dependent on the vibrato speed at all. The pulses can be mastered with a metronome at any speed. This makes a singer much more valuable to conductors who want to do more than one tempo during coloratura sections of an opera.

Once you have the previous examples down, move on to some bigger jumps in the voice. Next is an exercise that encompasses some octave work with both arpeggios on the way up with a dominant seven on the way down. Take this exercise up above the passaggio now as high as you can go (Example 9):

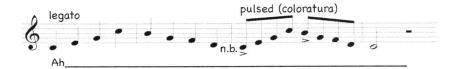

A breath should not be taken between the legato and coloratura parts of the exercises. That is the purpose of the exercises. Most music moves you abruptly into coloratura from legato in the same phrase and you need to know how to catapult into one. In fact, coloratura technique is used more often that you know. The time to use coloratura technique is any time the speed of the notes begins to get tangled with the vibrato speed--usually when you hit about eighty on the metronome (four sixteenth notes per click) and above. Sometimes you may only have two sixteenth notes in a phrase that use the technique. Adding the little pulse will clarify the pitches.

Once you have Example nine down to a science, move on to the next example with a long melismatic run of almost an octave and a half. Again, keep ascending by half steps until you reach the top of your range. Also remember that adjustments in laryngeal spacing are required on the way up and down all of these exercises (see the next chapter for a more thorough discussion). Here is Example 10:

With all of the examples here, this treatment of coloratura technique is only superficial. You need supervision to get the sound right, to make sure you are not singing in your throat, to make sure the pulse is affecting your pitch correctly, to make sure you are not working too hard or not enough, to make sure you are projecting your voice properly for the big stage, and to see if your vibrato is properly engaged during the process. It is difficult to monitor all of this without a teacher familiar with this technique.

Too many college graduates sing with messy melismas. Even sopranos who are traditionally coloratura sopranos often finish their schooling thinking they know how to sing "Rejoice" from *Messiah* (which they will do many, many times in their life) and have no clue how to sing cleanly and clearly so the audience can hear and perceive every single pitch.

Coloratura technique is used everywhere by every major composer somewhere in their operas. Just like physical fitness requires both strength and flexibility, so also does good opera singing require both strength and flexibility. The more skills you can put in your arsenal, the more valuable you will be to the opera world--and you will be able to take that to the bank.

Chapter 4

Vocal Registration

T oo many vocal departments at American colleges today are either governed by choral departments, or they are stuck in a combination of German and French school vocal ideals. If they follow these ideals, there will be an innate fear of discussing the factual physiological existence of vocal registers. Some are even in denial. Can singers deny the existence of registers and have a career? Perhaps, but only in small opera houses. Most of them become teachers. Surely there are exceptions to rules and some people sing correctly without knowing why they sing correctly.

Knowing how to sing well before studying voice seriously rarely helps singers achieve a career in opera. Why? First, because they naturally sing well, they don't know how the voice works. As a result, most do not know how to fix themselves when something goes wrong. If you didn't build your voice from scratch, you don't know how it works. In addition, most of these singers have no patience to reverse-engineer their voices in order to figure them out. Secondly, too many of them never had to work to achieve success in their singing and so they have no work ethic--especially the kind that it takes to have a career.

It is many of these types who become the teachers that are in denial about the physiological facts of the human voice and how it is put together. Others admit the physiological events that occur in the voice but are afraid to discuss them with their students for fear that the student will try to manipulate their voices in some unnatural ways. They also fear that the voice will also end up sounding artificial and manufactured. Unfortunately, for the majority of singers who don't come out of the womb singing "Nessun dorma," these fears will only keep them from an opera career.

An understanding of vocal registration is necessary to take the kinks out of the voice, to circumnavigate the breaks, to take pressure off the vocal cords and extend the time one can sing without vocal fatigue. In addition, it will make you sound better. For example, one of the worst vocal mistakes an operatic tenor can make is to sing a "g" above "middle c" on the wrong side of his register break. It's even worse when he is utterly unaware that he is doing it.

Some teachers teach a small bit of information about vocal registration, but neglect many of the basics. They approach upper registers through vowel modification which can work in some cases, but isn't precise enough, especially in music that is moving at high speed, like Rossini.

In addition to vowel modification, the German school tries to approach the biggest break in the voice (at the upper end of the passaggio) by attempting to artificially darken the voice as it approaches the register break in order to smoothly arrive on the opposite side of that break without drawing attention to it. The French school of voice generally tries to do this by increasing laryngeal spacing when approaching higher pitches, praying all the way to the top that their voices will "naturally" cross the breaks (which they never talk about) in all the right places. It is usually a vain supplication.

The Italians, on the other hand, not only unabashedly admit the existence of register breaks but keep the voice open before the break, and then cross into the next register cleanly in a way that may actually can draw attention to the existence of the break by the change in vocal color. This may be undesirable to the other schools, but it is the most natural and efficient way to sing and it also creates the most exciting sounds just below the break.

Let's begin with the basics about breaks. The voice is divided into different boxes called registers. The dividing lines between these boxes are called "register breaks." The Italians claim the existence of or focus on up to seven of these. Most important are the two largest and most obvious breaks in the voice. These two breaks are the boundaries of what is called the "passaggio" (or passageway). If the notes of the passiagio are in the right place, the rest of your voice usually works pretty well.

What so many choral people don't understand about vocal classification, is that what you are--meaning a lyric tenor, a spinto tenor, a dramatic baritone or a basso profundo--has little to do with your vocal "range" (how high or low you sing). It has everything to do with where your register breaks occur. Two people can have exactly the same range and one be a bass and one be a tenor based on where their breaks occur. It often takes some time in private voice lessons before your vocal classification can be determined. Before teachers can discover this, they have to make sure you are crossing your breaks in the natural places they were intended to be crossed.

Singers have the ability to cross register breaks in unnatural places. They can drag one register up too high and they can drag another down too low. When they cross incorrectly, their entire voice can be thrown out of alignment (sounding like they are singing too brightly or too darkly), and end up choking a quarter way through an opera. In fact, they may choke their high note in an aria for this reason. All too often singers or their teachers will blame the technical approach to a high note as the reason the high note didn't work. Often, the truth is that the singers have crossed a register break incorrectly two pages before the high note, getting out of alignment, and subsequently choking by the time they get to that high note. What happens before a high note is more important than the actual high note technique.

All people are born with their breaks in a different place. In other words, if my breaks make me a lyric tenor, then that is what and who I am no matter what my range. If, I audition for a role as a lyric tenor against a dramatic tenor, who has the same range, finesse, and stamina as I do, who will probably get the job? The dramatic tenor. Why? His voice will be more exciting on the same notes I sing. In other words, if I sing a "g" above "middle c" and so does the dramatic tenor, who has lower breaks than I do, the "g" will be more exciting from the dramatic tenor. If a baritone came in next and sang the "g" it would be even more exciting. However, the baritone would probably peter out before the end of the opera because of the tessitura. This is why stamina becomes a factor in hiring opera singers. Even the dramatic tenor will have a harder time than the lyric tenor getting through the opera.

This is why vocal classification exists. Rossini, Donizetti and Mozart operas often go to the lyric tenor because the tessitura is higher and will require less stamina of the lighter singer. What people don't know is that a lyric tenor can sing Siegfried or Otello more easily than a dramatic tenor. That isn't the reason he wouldn't be hired for these roles. Using his own voice, with higher register breaks, he wouldn't have the power of the dramatic tenor to project over the orchestra or over the soprano cast with him. This could also lead the lyric tenor to want to push and make his voice bigger and cause some damage. There are exceptions to all these rules, and from time to time a singer can do an exceptional job singing in a "fach" (the official word in opera meaning "vocal classification") that is not his own.

Where Are the Register Breaks?

Even though all people have their breaks in different places creating different vocal classifications, everyone's breaks are generally the same distance from one another and obey some basic rules. Dealing exclusively with the two largest breaks on both ends of the passaggio, here is a diagram of where these breaks occur in the lyric tenor voice on an "ah" vowel:

Just by way of explanation, the passaggio is sometimes spelled passagio (with one "g") depending on the books you read and schools you attend. The passaggio is also referred to by many as the "zona di passaggio" and by others as simply the passaggio. The biggest (often called the primary) break is often referred to as the "secondo passaggio" and the secondary break is often referred to as the "primo passagggio." This is because the Italians base the names on which one is lower and higher and not by which one is strongest and weakest. This can make things a bit confusing when discussing these things because they seem backwards. For the purposes of this book, the primo and secondo passaggi will be referred to as "breaks" and the zone or passageway between the two largest breaks will be called simply the passaggio.

You will notice that the large break in the above example occurs between F and G. You will also notice that the secondary break occurs down between the C and D. Why whole-steps and not half-steps? Because the F is clearly on one side of the break and the G is clearly on the other in this case. The F# is actually a kind of teeter-totter note and requires a kind of balancing act to be produced properly. Pavarotti was a master at this "teeter-totter" note and felt that if you got these notes right in an aria, the rest of the aria would work itself out. Many felt his F#s were even better and more exciting to listen to than his "high Cs."

If your breaks are a half step lower than the above example, you may be a spinto tenor. If it is another half step lower, a dramatic tenor. That is how it works. The distance between the bigger break at the top and the smaller one at the bottom generally remains the same--about a perfect fourth.

Now for those that discuss and embrace the existence of register breaks, one thing that not adequately discussed, even in the best books, is the fact that register breaks change depending on what vowel you are singing. This is important to understand in order to have a complete understanding of the phenomenon. Let's stick with the lyric tenor breaks for purposes of the discussion (the lyric soprano breaks a pretty much one octave above the lyric tenor). Let's also deal with the five Italian vowels. Using international phonetic symbols we have already established the breaks of the [ɑ] to be:

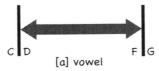

[ɑ] vowel

Using Italian vowels, the [o] and the [e] have the same breaks as one another and they are one whole step below the [ɑ] vowel as indicated below:

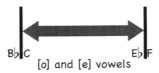

[o] and [e] vowels

The [i] and the [u] are another whole step down below the [o] and [e] vowels as shown here:

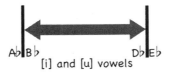

[i] and [u] vowels

Why do the breaks move when the vowel changes? You can see why more clearly by taking a look at the common diction vowel triangle here:

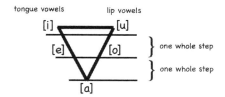

You'll notice that the vowel with the same breaks are on the same vertical placement on both sides of the vowel triangle (i.e., the [o] is directly across from the [e] and the [i] from the [u]). This reflects the degree to which the vowel is closed. The vowels on the left side of the triangle represent the "tongue vowels"--meaning the vowel is slowly closed as the back of the tongue rises and closes the vowel. The vowels on the right side of the triangle represent the "lip vowels"--meaning that vowels are closed by bringing the lips around and slowly closing off the vowel. The vertical placement of the vowels corresponds directly to the degree to which the vowels are closed.

The purpose of this book is not to be a book on IPA symbols or vocal diction. If you want to chart out the breaks in your voice, get yourself a diction book that shows pictures of the vowel triangle in all of the different languages in which you sing. Many books have mapped out exactly where the vowels of a particular language belong on the triangle that will, in turn, help you to map out your register breaks.

Too many singers, who think they understand vocal registration, have the misguided opinion that their breaks stay in a consistent place for all vowels. This can get them into a lot of trouble when they start singing opera. This can almost be as bad as the singers who are hiding or ignoring the existence of their register breaks in the German and French schools.

If you are going to know your voice, you need to understand your vocal registers. Professionals know their voices inside and out. They know them vowel to vowel and note to note. Once you understand where your voice naturally crosses its breaks, you can mark your music as a reminder to cross in important places--especially fast sections and melismas where you will be more likely to make a crossing mistake.

Register crossing mistakes are easier to make than you might think. They happen all the time. This is not just because of bad vocal habits, but because breaks are subtle. Even the best singers incorrectly cross their breaks every once in a while.

Vocal registration is also directly related to laryngeal spacing. This is actually one of the ways other national schools come close to achieving the right sound. In order to maintain "sameness" (the goal of all classical training), laryngeal spacing must be increased as singers move to higher pitches. Adding or decreasing laryngeal space is also a method by which one crosses register breaks.

Although many schools of thought teach singers to increase this spacing for higher pitches, the methodology is often quite imprecise. This is because they don't explain to you exactly how much space is required for each pitch. Each pitch requires an exact amount of laryngeal space depending on the vowel you are singing. As pitch goes down, so also should your laryngeal spacing decrease. In spite of the meticulousness this implies, it should be emphasized that this is not manipulated, but must be natural to your particular body. You need to find the natural amount of space required for each pitch and each vowel so that your body can sing freely and efficiently. Too much space creates artificial darkness to your tone and too little space creates too much brightness to the tone (an often a strangled sound). Both of these mistakes create vocal tension and will tire out your voice over time. You cannot be something you are not. If you try to be, you can even cause damage. Healthy singing requires that you find the natural spacing of for each vowel and pitch.

There are times you will manipulate the laryngeal spacing for coloring purposes or dramatic reasons. However, the coloring is a choice and not the norm. Understanding the spacing requirements of an efficiently produced sound should be the developed habit and coloring should be the artistic choice.

Because vocal registration works together with laryngeal spacing, it is important to point out that the amount of space required corresponds directly to the position of the register breaks. What this means is that for the lyric tenor example above, a "G" requires as much laryngeal spacing (and support) on an [ɑ] vowel as is required for E-flat on a [i] vowel. And it means that the spacing required for that [i] vowel on that "E-flat" has the same difficulty as an [o] vowel on the note "F."

To make things even more complicated, schools often teach the application of breath support to these vowel and pitch issues with the same imprecision. They tell you that high notes require more support. But do they tell you how much? Just like the laryngeal spacing is incremental, so also is the support mechanism. The higher the note, the more support is required. The lower the note, the less. Too much support on a note causes the singer to push and put too much pressure on the cords and too little causes you to sing in your throat. Both will never get you through an opera.

So let's recap this so far: As notes go higher, support and laryngeal space must increase to a perfect natural amount for your particular body and as the notes go lower, the support and spacing must decrease to the same degrees. As vowels change, support and laryngeal spacing must make changes as well. If I am on an "F" and I change vowels from an [a] vowel to an [i] vowel, I must increase my support even though I am staying on the same note. In fact, I must increase that support by exactly that which is required to go up two whole steps in pitch because of the requirements of vocal registration. The more closed the vowel the more support and laryngeal spacing is required to sing that note, even if it is on the same pitch.

Again, most schools and teachers ignore this. And yet, it is how the physiology works. The problem with the imprecision of many vocal methods is that singers don't become aware of subtleties in space and support. In addition, the imprecision allows singers to cross their breaks either too early or too late on ascending or descending passages. Rossini singers, in particular, cannot afford this kind of messiness, because they have four times as many notes to sing as a Verdi or Puccini singer. It's far too easy to make registration mistakes when singing though quick passage work. This can throw you off and choke you right in the middle of an aria. You see this happen all too often with people preparing for high notes. They are singing high, go low, then need to pop back up for a high note and choke. What happened? Often they had a lot of laryngeal space for the high note but didn't decrease their space and support when they went to the lower notes, but instead dragged down the space required for the high note down to the low note. When they try to ascend again, they are already at full distention of the larynx and they choke.

Precision in your technique and a complete familiarity with what your voice and body does on every note and every vowel is paramount for a professional opera singer. You can spend a lifetime mastering these things. You cannot afford to take risks with your voice, hoping that you will happen to land on the right side of a break by casually throwing unspecified degrees of space and support at the desired pitch. Singing is not for the faint of heart, and it is not something you decide to do because you are too lazy to become a lawyer or a doctor. It is science and it is art and it is complex. Don't be fooled into thinking anything else. Prepare for your career like a scientist and then you will be free and have the tools necessary to become an artist.

Chapter 5

Language and Diction

Just a very few words about language and diction need to be said here. There is certainly a great deal of entertainment value in watching a soprano sing to her beloved car when singing "O mio babbino caro." It's also more than embarrassing when a tenor is singing to Violetta in *La Traviata* sings "ah si, da un anno" without the proper doppio on "anno." Sopranos may not intend to sing "carro" rather than "caro", but a frightening number of college graduates sing this new, rather humorous song because they weren't taught simple rules of diction, like when to sing a rolled "R."

Again, although it is tempting to get into diction issues (like single-tapping an "R" between vowels in the same word), this book is not a diction book. There are many wonderful diction books out there. Also, one of the few nice things this book will say about schools is that most of them teach fairly good classes on IPA symbols. However, it must also be said, that if you don't get a 4.0 or an "A" in the IPA classes, you need to take them again, if you intend on becoming an opera singer. You need IPA classes in English, Italian,

Latin, German, and French. If schools go the extra mile, they might add Russian, Spanish, Portuguese, and Czech.

As a professional opera singer you can try to depend on coaches to correct your diction during your career, but what you are doing is hiding behind your coach. There will be times when you will be asked to read something in front of someone important and they will know right then and there if you sound like a native or you do not. If you aren't at least close, you won't be hired back. That's how important it is in the opera world (unfortunately, Europeans and Asians are not expected to have the same degree of pronunciation proficiency when singing in English as Americans are expected to have in their languages).

In fact, it's more important than mere pronunciation. You have to speak the languages too. Most vocal programs require at least one semester of Italian, French and German. The purpose for this is to teach you, at the very least, how to use a dictionary, and how to conjugate the verbs. You can get a small foundation by following this curriculum. However, it's not enough. You need to be at least semi-fluent in these languages. If you cannot get by in one of these countries after losing your Fodor's phrasebook, you haven't learned enough.

Why do you need to learn to speak these languages? First, if you are going to make a living, you will sing in Europe--at least from time to time. Your directors and colleagues will all speak these languages. In the big houses in America, you will also, from time to time, have stage directors, conductors, and singers that don't speak English. But these are logistical reasons.

More important to your art is the fact that you will be expected to act in the language in which you are singing. You will need to know exactly what every word means that is coming out of your mouth and make it look as if you are thinking in the language, not simply regurgitating a few lessons in diction. Imagine for a moment what it is like when people come to your country and try to say something in English phonetically without understanding a word they are saying. Not only is the diction off, but there is an associated blank stare. Don't think for a minute that you look and come off any differently when you don't speak the language in which you are singing. It's obvious to everyone in the business. Also, don't be surprised if you are stopped during a rehearsal by a director who perceives this and asks you what you just said or what a specific word means. This will happen.

In addition, the audience will know, especially the high-paying ones. Each opera audience has different sections. You may have spent twenty-five dollars to get your nosebleed seats, but some spend thousands for their box seats. They expect the most perfect performance the opera company can provide. There are many people in the audience that know every word of the opera without the need for supertitles. Many of these people are the very donors that keep the opera company alive. You miss a word, they know. You look like you don't know what you are saying, they know. They will talk about it with other wealthy donors, and they will talk with the manager of the opera company, and you will not work there again.

The biggest surprise to most young opera singers is the degree of perfection that is required as they move to larger opera houses with bigger budgets. It may seem like an almost a non-human perfection at times. If you do not speak the languages, you will be competing against people who do.

So, start with the diction, because you not only need to understand the language, but you need to sound like a native. Find a coach who will beat you up for every nuance of diction. Remember, like your teachers, you don't pay them to clap their hands and tell you how wonderful you are. Opera is a hybrid art form that incorporates many other art forms. Language is just one of them. The natural flow and diction of the language is what originally inspired the composer to write his or her music. Therefore, respect its importance in your career. Remember, your goal is not to sing at small opera companies the rest of your life.

Chapter 6

Breathing and Support

We only need to discuss a few matters on breath management. This, of course, is the foundational element of singing and should have been the first thing you were taught in any school. Unlike many other techniques of singing, it is the first thing you learn and the last thing you learn. In the end, you are still working on the subtleties of support because you realize the support is foundational and controls so many other vocal techniques.

Different schools teach support in different ways. Some methods promote everything from "squeezing the dime" (between your fanny cheeks) to actually using the defecatory muscles. Although the connection of these muscles to the lungs is yet to be determined (not to mention that it makes it tough to walk naturally on stage), what is important is the ability to project and sustain in a true Italianate *appoggio*.

In Pavarotti's book, *My Own Story*, the great tenor stated that a steady stream of singers would set appointments to come sing for him in his dressing room before a performance, hoping to get "discovered." The amusing thing is that time after time he would send them away with the same advice: Work on your support. It's always the same problem.

During an audition, this is one of the most obvious problems among singers--a basic understanding of how to manage the breath. It manifests itself in many ways. Many times, it's in the fact that the singer cannot get through a single sentence in one breath. Most singers don't even know that they are supposed to get through a single thought in a single breath and some even breathe in the middle of words.

If you can't hold a strong note for at least thirty seconds, you don't completely understand support. This may sound like an arbitrary number, but not really--it is a quite common benchmark. Many professionals can hold them for a minute. The benchmark during the baroque period among singers was eight measures. If you are singing a long melismatic phrase in Händel, you need to get through it and its associated sentence in one breath, whether it is "Rejoice" from *Messiah* or "So shall the lute and harp awake." (By the way, every singer should learn Händel's melismatic arias as a lesson in basic technique.)

In addition, volume should not affect support negatively. Louder singing most often requires less air than more. If you don't understand this, you also don't understand support. Too many singers approach a loud section of their aria and suddenly are gasping for breath during an audition.

Another obvious lack during an audition is a lack of control over vibrato because of uneven support. Sometimes the vibrato stops and starts at will or speeds up as the singer approaches higher pitches--a sure sign of a lack of understanding of how support needs to be adjusted with pitch.

Support is not about "tightening the tummy" or holding on to muscles at one single pressure throughout a phrase. Many singers get out of school without having been taught that there are TWO muscle groups responsible for breath support--those responsible for inhaling and those responsible for exhaling. These two sets of muscle must resist one another for proper support. When the support changes, as it does when changing pitch and vowels, both sets of muscles must be incrementally added or taken away. You do not just tighten more or less.

The abdominals (the exhaling muscles) are much stronger in general than the diaphragm (responsible for inhalation). As such, if both sets are working evenly against one another, it will feel as if the diaphragm is working harder, because it is weaker. Read that again if you didn't get it. The stronger a muscle is, the less you feel it when it is working. This is why so many describe support as a feeling of inspiration or expansion. Now, part of maintaining balance between the muscles requires an understanding of the strength of your particular muscles. As your diaphragm increases in strength as you develop it, you will have to make adjustments based on this understanding.

Another problem many beginning students of the voice have when learning how to support is in the use of sympathetic muscles. What this means is that many people have habits or dispositions to use muscles that have nothing to do directly with the control of the breath, but that like to be used at the same time as the natural breathing muscles. For example, some singers will use the natural support muscles properly, but will simultaneously tighten other muscles like the hands, the neck, the shoulders, or muscles of the face. These sympathetic issues can go the other way as well, in that some singers can only support if they first use muscles (like those of the buttocks) that have nothing to do with the lungs. It is sure that these muscles can psychologically help singers through sympathetic means, but ultimately, the use of sympathetic muscles to get things going can get in the way.

Your understanding of breath support will control not only your vibrato, but your phrasing, your use of coloratura technique, your methodology of diction, your correct use of vocal registration, you legato technique, your tone quality, and your vocal freedom. If you don't get this right to begin with, you're going to compromise your ability to execute these other techniques.

Work on the mechanisms of the breath must be a priority, even for the advanced singer. Subtle changes in the use of the support muscles can affect great beauty and control and add to your value and employability as a singer. Learn about your support meticulously. Know the exact amount of support that is required for each pitch and each vowel so that when you sing, you don't wonder what is going to come out of your mouth--you know.

Chapter 7

Performance Practice

Not a lot is taught to the undergraduate student of voice regarding performance practice. There are many fabulous books on this subject written on this subject. There are many great books written on the performance practices of just about every major composer of opera. Studying this subject should be a lifelong endeavor.

One of the naïve ideas that too many new graduates believe is that because they see a note on the page, they can just perform it the way they perform any other note in any other piece of music. It would be great if big name music publishers, who seem to have no qualms in editing up a score so that half of what you see was never written by the composer, would edit it in such a way as to reflect performance practice. Unfortunately, many of these big companies themselves hire people to edit and transcribe from original manuscripts who do not understand the basics of the performance practices associated with that composer.

Here is a brief example from the aria, "Come scoglio" from a Schirmer score of *Cosi fan tutte*:

You will notice that fermatas have been inserted in Fiordiligi's line. But here is what Mozart actually wrote in his score:

These weren't fermatas at all. These huge signs which resemble fermatas were actually intended as directions to the singer to ornament or write their own intermediate cadenzas. Thanks to wonderful books like that of Frederick Neumann, *Ornamentation and Improvisation in Mozart*, for example, we can better understand what Mozart intended when he wrote anything. In this book, there are numerous examples of Mozart's own words and examples pointing out what he expected to hear his singer do when he wrote something on the page.

Here is the same passage as edited by Kalmus:

You can see that Kalmus tried to put a fermata in between notes in the first measure (without explaining what it meant) and then used phrase marks over the other measures.

The editors at Kalmus and especially Schirmer didn't do their homework, and so we have a fermata in the above examples (and many other scores of Mozart operas). But what's worse, singers get out of college and are singing these examples as fermatas because they don't know any better or are not taught any better.

So what are singers left with? Because they weren't taught these things as undergraduates, they go out into the world and pass misinformation along. In fact, many of them start engaging in what is called circular sourcing. This is like the blind leading the blind. They copy incorrect interpretations of others. In fact, many teachers and coaches out there actually use recordings as a primary source of how to interpret a score.

Irene Dalis, at one time the highest paid mezzo-soprano in the world, tells an interesting story of making her recording of Wagner's *Parsifal* before the days of digital editing. After recording a lengthy scene, she realized she had made a mistake with a particular phrase and asked to record the entire section over. Because of the cost of studio time, orchestra time, and other considerations, they told her they couldn't redo the recording. So, to this day, the mistake is on her recording. But this isn't the best part of the story. Later, she tells of going to the MET to hear her successor sing the role, and there was her mistake, unmistakably sung by the leading mezzo, obviously emulating the great diva.

Do we learn what is in the score based on what the composer intended, or do we follow the examples of others lucky enough to get recording contracts? If you are going to learn a score, try to learn it without hearing the opera first and after doing your homework. Then later, listen to others who have recorded it for interpretational ideas.

Once you understand performance practice, your view of music will suddenly change as well. Composers were and are terribly limited by the constraints of notation, meter, and dynamic markings that don't accurately portray the freedom you have in interpretation. Mozart would have expected ornaments different than Rossini; Puccini portamenti differ from those of Verdi; The dotted rhythms of Verdi and Händel are more double dotted than single dotted; Baroque dotted rhythms can be used to infer a triplet rhythm if triplets are used elsewhere in the piece; cadenzas are supposed to be in one breath, not the silly, self- indulgent, never ending multiple-breath cadenzas performed by those making fun of the opera world. (If you can't do a cadenza in one breath, don't do it, get another aria, or work on your technique.)

Now, certainly there is a great deal of tradition that has accumulated over the years in opera that becomes so popular, you almost cannot get a job unless you are willing to put performance practice aside and follow the tradition. Examples might be, the "high C" at the end of "Di quella pira" in *Il Trovatore*, or the High E-flat at the end of "Sempre libera" in *La Traviata*. Of course, you don't have to take that high note if you are Renée Fleming, and you can take "Che gelida manina" down a step if you are Luciano Pavarotti. But making a living is different than being a superstar. Superstars don't always have to keep the same rules as those who do this day in and day out. For the rest of the opera singers in the world, you have to sing those notes to get your job. If you can't, you'll be competing against those that can.

Traditionally, as mentioned before, at the end of a slow section of a Verdi bel canto aria, the final note will be held to cut off with the orchestra and just before the cut off, the singer's vibrato will be expected to speed up. Sometimes a tradition can result from the need for another tradition. For example, quite often when a traditional high note is coming at the end of an aria, it also becomes a tradition to give the singer a break by doing a "tacit," meaning NOT singing the notes for a couple of bars before the high note.

As a singer, you need to learn how to navigate your way between performance practices and traditions and discard the erroneous interpretations of singers who think they are doing what the composer intended when, in fact, they are not.

How to Sing Recitative

Nothing is more of a mess among young singers than their recitative. There are a few schools that seem to get this right, but not near enough. So, here are a few things you need to understand and a few rules you need to keep in putting together a recitative:

1. Understand to begin with that recitatives are the meat and potatoes of bel canto opera. The story takes place during the recitative and the arias and ensembles comment on the story. It is similar to musical theater, where the story takes place with the dialogue and the songs comment on the dialogue.

2. Understand that the recitative is NOT the aria. It should not be sung like one under any circumstances, no matter what kind of recitative it is.

3. There are two basic kinds of recitative: "secco" (or dry recit) and "accompagnato" (or accompanied recit). The secco recitative is usually, but not always, accompanied by some kind of continuo or keyboard instrument. The accompanist follows the singer in general. The accompagnato recitative is usually accompanied by the orchestra, and the singer must keep his tempi in line with the conductor and orchestra for the most part. In some cases, there are secco recits (the words "recit" and "recits" are the jargon used in the business) that are accompanied by the orchestra and accompagnato sections played by the keyboard. Keep your eyes open for these differences.

4. When doing dry recit, please understand that the rests were not put in for you to take a breath. They were put there to delineate either harmonic phrasing or melodic impetus, sometimes requiring simple lilts in the phrase without a breath. Most times, especially according to tradition, just cross the rests out that are not separating thoughts or sentences and express the full thought or sentence in one single breath.

5. When doing dry recit, begin by saying the words at the speed of a fluent Italian. The recit should be generally performed at spoken speed. Does this mean one speed? No. When we speak, we pause, lilt, speed up and slow down. Learn to speak naturally, based on the excitement or current feelings of the character you are portraying. The composer sometimes helps this along by writing notes that are longer than others to give you and idea (and only an idea) of which notes should be a bit longer than the others. Dry recit is not to be counted or metered. A string of eighth notes, for example, are not to be sung evenly.

6. When you add pitches to your full-speed spoken dialogue in dry recit, make sure they are not generally straight-tone. There should be a "vibrato quality" behind the notes in spite of their extreme speed. Remember this is not an aria, but the voice and connection to the body must be there. When people speak normally, they don't generally support or connect, but you need to do this when you make the transition from speaking the Italian words to adding the notes.

7. Get off the endings. Another thing that makes the dry recit sound like dialogue is the way that you lift off of the final note of each phrase. You should never hold the final note of a phrase of recit, unless demanded by the composer. Most dry recit phrases end in an eighth note and is intended to even be shorter than that. In addition, most of these phrases end in appoggiaturas. Appoggiaturas are sometimes referred to as "almost notes." When singing, the appoggiatura is emphasized and often the climax of a phrase and the following note is dramatically reduced in volume and lifted off of quickly.

8. Much recitative contains inferred appoggiaturas, meaning that the appoggiatura is not spelled out, but generally expected. Here is an example of a written appoggiatura in an aria (un aura amorosa):

In recitative, however, what you will see is two notes written at the end of the phrase exactly on the same pitch. It was intended that the penultimate note be different. The ending decorations of phrases were left up to the singer. Sometimes, the appoggiatura can be approached from beneath the note, and sometimes from above. Generally, if the note before the appoggiatura is below then the singer chooses an appoggiatura note below as well. The same for above. But this is not required--tradition only. Here is an example (from the recit right before "un aura amorosa"):

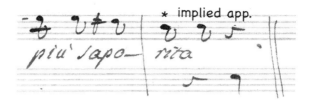

In performance, the note with the asterisk would be a note higher (or even lower) by inference.

9. Recitativo accompagnato, is different in that the singer has to accommodate melodic motifs and metered orchestra. This means that the composer wanted more control over the speeds and accompanying dramatic intent of the recitative. However, too many coaches and singers have overreached in these recits and perform them at the speed of the arias themselves. They were never intended to be this way.

Generally good examples of properly performed recit can be heard in recordings of Rossini operas. Unfortunately, there are far to many recordings of Verdi operas where you can hear all kinds of incorrect recitative, especially because some coaches and teachers mistakenly believe that all Verdi recit is "accompagnato" in style because the recit is accompanied by the orchestra. Much of it, especially the pre-verismo bel canto operas of Verdi, is secco style recitative accompanied by orchestra. It is secco when the need for conducting a strict rhythm is unnecessary and chords are held, allowing the singer to sing at free tempi. It is written and delivered much the same way as earlier recits accompanied by a continuo. It needs to be somewhat slower than Rossini recitative but still performed at spoken speed--and nothing like the aria itself.

Other kinds of recits that are improperly performed are those in oratorio. There are too many conductors coming on the scene who don't know their ictus from a preparatory gesture, and they take on choral music without understand the recitative. Since most of the recitatives in oratorio are Classical or pre-Classical, they need to be executed much like Rossini recitatives. To date, most of the time, singers still sing these recits like arias, and don't get off their endings, but hold the final notes in either self-indulgence or ignorance.

Final Words on Performance Practice

If your school offers a performance practice class, take it, even if it is not required. Of course, if you are going to school to get a diploma and not an education, then forget it. Unfortunately, most schools that offer classes in performance practice don't have a separate class for the performance practice of opera. You may have to wade through Bach ornamentation and symphonic literature. Check into it at your school.

Otherwise, start building your library by ordering books on performance practice for the primary composers of opera--especially those in your repertory. There are many out there. Believe in yourself enough to study things that are not required by any curriculum. Success in this business, or any business for that matter, is dependent on your willingness to continually make yourself more valuable. That value translates into a viable career as a singer who can be trusted to do his or her homework and not need to be corrected by conductors and directors.

This is a great opportunity for you to stand out from the crowd of other singers who haven't reached out for knowledge beyond that which is required to obtain a diploma. There is a sea of mediocre college graduates who will come to an audition without this knowledge. But nothing is more impressive that listening to a singer audition who ornaments and interprets like a professional.

Chapter 8

Preparing the score

Y ou will have to learn and memorize a great deal of music in your life. Learning how to memorize is an important skill. You are not only memorizing the music (notes and rhythm), but also the words in a foreign language, the expression, the staging, and the subtext. You have so much to remember that you do not have time to think about it all while you are on stage. Your technique must be automatic. This means that you must sing correctly without thinking about it. You simply will not have time to concentrate on your technique during an opera. The more techniques that you make second nature, the more space you will free up in your brain. It's hard enough for some people to pat their heads and rub their stomachs at the same time, let alone juggle all of the hundreds of techniques that simultaneously must be employed by and opera singer. So, the trick is to make it all habitual.

As you prepare a score for performance, you will have much to think about. If you just memorize your notes, you will have some difficulty later when you try to add the expression and acting. This is because of the principle of muscle memory.

Understand now that whatever technique you have or use when you memorize a song is the same technique that will come out when you perform. This is because you are memorizing much more than the notes, rhythms and words. You are memorizing the whole experience. All the muscles used by your body are being memorized along with the music itself. This is why your voice teacher sometimes discourages you from learning certain repertoire too soon.

If you learn an operatic aria that will be your bread and butter in your life before you have your technique in place, you will be stuck with that technique for years to come. When your technique is ready years later, you will go to sing that song and all of the old, inferior technique will come flooding back--even against your will. If this happens, you will have to play some mind tricks to relearn your song from scratch. You will need to look at the notes as if you had never seen them before. It is very hard to undo muscle memory. So you want to do it right from the start.

If you learn a song without the expression, it will be harder to paste it onto pre-memorized notes and rhythms. Learn them together. If you memorize a song singing half-voice (so you don't wake up your neighbors), you will find that your memory will fail you when you try to sing full voice. This is also why singers, at rehearsal, forget their words the minute that the stage director asks them to act on top of their music. In addition, if you come to rehearsal with a concept of your character and the stage director changes that character, you can also forget your music. This is why you must over-memorize so that you can deal with any modifications that you will be asked to make. You need to be able to do the dishes or do summersaults without losing a beat in your music. Try do distract yourself and see if the memory sticks.

Study memory techniques. There are many--every things from chaining techniques to pegging techniques. There are books and tapes on the subject. The better you are at memorizing, the more valuable you will be in the opera world. More singers than you know get their big break when someone gets sick and you have three days to memorize an entire leading role. Can you do it?

In addition, can you do it in a foreign language? All good memorizing begins with understanding every word of the opera. Professional singers do not just translate their parts, but they translate everyone else's. You must know what everyone is saying in the opera. When someone is speaking to you, you cannot just nod and pretend you know what they just said to you.

Phrasing and Expression

There is nothing that sets you apart more during an audition that an absolute control over your phrasing and expression. The decisions you make regarding interpretation, which include your knowledge of performance practice, are some of the principal judgments that will get you jobs. Imagine sitting through auditions all day, listening to one singer after another who all sing the right words, the right notes, and the correct rhythms. This is exactly what happens. Then suddenly a singer comes in who can do more than robotically regurgitate what is in the opera score, but expresses an original feeling or interpretation based on musical and dramatic subtext.

You need to understand that an audition is a performance. If you see those you are singing for as simply adjudicators, you will be missing the mark. They actually desire to be artistically fed just like any future audience member. If you treat the audition as a performance and feed them, you will get the job. If, on the other hand, you see the experience as if you were going to court, it will show in your performance.

A robot can sing the notes, rhythms and words. It's what you do with those three things that make music. As an opera singer, you must learn how to create a phrase. Where does your phrase go? If you can't answer that question about every single phrase you sing, then you are not ready to sing in public. Most good composers set up your music to answer this question for you. Generally, the answer is this: the final downbeat of the last measure of the phrase. While this is not always the case, it is most of the time.   Here's another Mozart example:

In this example, you will notice the exact syllable to which the phrase should crescendo, and from which it should decrescendo. This is shape. Composers expect that you know how to do this, and so they don't bother writing in the microscale crescendos and decrescendos in the music. Instead, most of them just put a general dynamic marking and then expect that the experienced performer will not just sing one volume throughout the section.

Unlike the piano, the voice can crescendo while holding a note. When phrasing on a piano, the pianist can execute a crescendo by making each note louder than the last. The voice can create a better phrase by having each note be part of the larger crescendo within itself. And yet, so many singers, trained alongside pianos, imitate the piano in changing dynamics note by note. Once you add legato or portamento technique, you will have a phrase that is superior to anything created by any other instrument.

This ability to sing "horizontally" was so exciting to composers that they wrote music that would showcase this ability. This music today is often referred to as "bel canto" music (corresponding to bel canto technique). During the period that composers wrote this music, they would create a smooth vocal melody that would be sung horizontally accompanied by the stark contrast of a vertical accompaniment--what many refer affectionately to as an "um-pah-pah" accompaniment. Unfortunately, many singers misunderstand the point of bel canto music and, mesmerized by the um-pah-pah, sing vertically with the accompaniment, joining with the fun, but destroying the intended contrast.

Another expressive skill heard in professionals is demonstrated in the way they handle their crescendos and phrasal climaxes. Beginning singers are tempted to speed up as they crescendo through a phrase. Professionals know that they are not metronomes. They slow up slightly as they approach a climax. They hang on just a tad to the note right before the climax and build anticipation. The climax performed this way has much more power than a simple crescendo and gives the illusion of having gotten louder. Harpsichordists use this technique with their articulation techniques to give the illusion of a crescendo even though the plectrums can only create one volume.

Experienced performers also know how to deftly handle ornaments and cadenzas. In general, ornaments are never intended to be sung evenly. Here is the basic rule: Slow-Fast-slow. This will give you some basic shape to the ornament or cadenza. Let's say that you are executing a trill. Start slow, speed up in the middle, and then slow out of it (sometimes with a lower turn). You can do the same thing with a melismatic cadenza. Start the run slowly on the first two or three notes, speed up to a coloratura technique, and then slow out of the run during the last couple of notes. You can learn to decorate and be playful in this way, experimenting with your shaping further. Here is an example from "O del mio dolce ardor" from the famous Twenty-Four Italian aria book:

Now, here is one general way it can be performed according to the Slow-Fast-Slow rule (again, the note values are not exact):

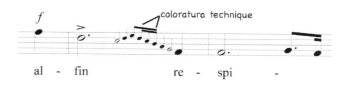

Even the second example is limited by the requirements of notation and cannot really represent what you should execute with its gradual increases and decreases in velocity. Composers are always limited by the constraints of notes, rhythms, tempi, and meter and cannot always adequately explain actual performance practice. This is why you not only need to study performance practice, but also need to listen to singers execute these ideas.

When creating phrases, it is important for you to understand that every phrase you sing is part of a larger phrase, which is in turn part of a still larger one, often encompassing the whole song. Even the entire opera has its own harmonic and dramatic climaxes. You need to know where these places are and how to execute them.

When you create a phrase, you need to take away all doubt. Don't leave the audience wondering if your dynamic changes were intended. Make a big enough contrast from the beginning of the phrase to the climax and then another contrast between the climax and any additional remaining notes. Make a phrase stand out. Don't be abrupt in these dynamic changes, but be absolutely even and don't change the nature of the vibrato or your tone along the way. Phrases require finesse and a great deal of practice and control. But they are worth your time. They will get you your jobs and set you apart from other singers who don't take the time to make artistic choices.

As you learn your music and prepare your scores, learn them meticulously and learn them correctly the first time so you establish the correct muscle memory. After a while, learning future scores correctly will become easier and require less time. Habits can only be created by doing things slowly, methodically, and regularly with a great deal of concentration. Once the habit is established whether it be how to shape a phrase, execute a trill, or memorize words in a foreign language, it will become second nature and you can move on to focusing on your acting or even more important artistic decisions.

Chapter 9

Acting

I f you think opera is just about music or singing, you need to get out of the dark ages (which some affectionately call the golden age of singing). In these heady times, singers were omnipotent, and it was enough to see them stand on the stage in a pretty dress in a prepackaged posture.

Opera is and always was intended to be a hybrid of art forms. It was never meant to be oratorio. When you buy a CD, you are only experiencing half of the art form (or maybe less). This is every bit as much an acting genre as it is a music genre--especially today. Audiences of today demand character development, dramatic nuance, and theatrical subtext from their singers.

If this book were true to this ideal, it would be more evenly split between music and acting. But the truth is, you need an entire book (or more) on acting. Most young singers need the basics because acting of any kind is rarely required or even offered by any opera program in any school. Too many singers think acting and blocking are the same things. This is probably the biggest gap between schools and the business of opera that there is.

There are basically two kinds of stage directors you will work with in opera companies. Let's briefly describe them.

1. <u>Pretty Picture Directors.</u> They want the stage to look balanced and put you into beautiful positions on stage. As a result, you, as an actor, need to make moving into those positions look spontaneous and natural. The acting is, in fact, less spontaneous and natural. Most directors in opera will be this way, however, because they feel you will be constrained by the music anyway. Opera singers tend to learn to be pretty good at this kind of acting, even better than many straight actors. (By "straight actors" we mean non-singing stage actors).

2. <u>Acting Directors.</u> These directors often come from theaters that do actual plays and work with legitimate actors. They will discuss character and motivation, and then they will let you roam free on the stage. This means that they will expect your movements and acting to come from a place motivated by your character and its spontaneous interactions with others on stage. This is very disconcerting to many singers unfamiliar with straight acting. Most singers like to be told where to stand.

There is a third kind of director you will work with from time to time--the bad director. Yes, there are a lot of wannabe directors out there that have no sense of motivation and also have no sense of movement and the needs of an opera singer. Smile, say "yes sir," and do your best with the little you will be given. They will often tell you to sing sideways or upstage, they will never discuss your character, and they will generally come unprepared to a rehearsal--making it all up as they go along.

This book can spell out some of the basics you will need to get by in the opera world, but if you have never had an acting class of any kind, you may need to take one. Understand that acting is not an easier skill or art form than singing. People also get advanced degrees in acting. However, acting has to be slightly modified for the opera stage. Much of true acting doesn't take kindly to the constraints of the meter, tempo, and rhythms spelled out in music. So some accommodations have to be made.

Constraints of Acting for Opera

To begin with, before we can get into acting, understand that because there are no microphones in opera (legitimate opera), your voice needs to go out to the audience. If it goes sideways into the wings, the voice will disappear. Therefore, while you are singing you cannot generally turn your head more than forty-five degrees in either direction. This is a limitation that most straight actors do not have. Most of them do not worry about the nuances of tone and projection that are required in opera. They also don't have to say their lines over an orchestra.

However, the eyes do not have this limitation. You can look about another forty-five degrees further with the eyes than the head should turn as an opera singer. As a result, there is a pattern used by many opera singers today of how to add a perceived forty-five degrees to both sides of your acting field. Here is a picture to help describe what this looks like.

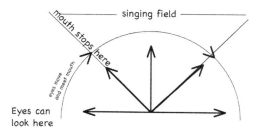

AUDIENCE

As you can see, the eyes are at ninety degrees, then move to meet the head at the forty-five degree mark, then both eyes and head can move together to the other side and although the head stops at forty-five degrees on the other side, the eyes can continue moving after that another forty-five degrees. Try this as an exercise back and forth a number of times. In the beginning, it will feel a bit awkward and even unnatural. It certainly will seem repellent to the straight actor. However, as an opera singer you can learn to feel quite natural about this. In a way, all you have to think about is keeping your mouth connected to your audience. Do what you will with the rest of your body.

Now, once you've dealt with this constraint, you need to know how to deal with other people on stage. If you haven't learned the difference between downstage and upstage, "stage left" and "stage right," let's just review the basics:

Up Stage Right	Up Stage Center	Up Stage Left
Stage Right	Center Stage	Stage Left
Down Stage Right	Down Stage Center	Down Stage Left

Audience

First, know that anytime you are not singing or the score indicates a section of rests, you can turn upstage all you want. In fact, it can look good if you have extended rests. However, this can look bizarre if you have only a few rests and you are taking turns singing to a partner on stage. You do not want to look upstage and then suddenly turn downstage every time it is your turn to sing in these kinds of sections. You need to get over one thing--the idea that you must look at the person to whom you are singing on stage. This is one of the worst mistakes singers make.

Another mistake that too many inexperienced singers make is in standing parallel to a partner with whom they are singing. One should generally be upstage of the other. Never stand parallel to another singer on stage, move upstage or downstage of them, depending on what is appropriate. Again, if you are obsessed with seeing the person to whom you are singing, you will have a problem. If you were in a room being thoughtful while speaking to someone else, you would feel no need to directly look at them. This is what you can do on stage as well. You know they are in the room and can speak to them without looking.

So what are you looking at then? Nothing. There are two basic kinds of focus on stage--internal and external. Having an external focus means you are looking at something tangible and specific on stage. An internal focus means you are thinking internally, contemplating ideas, or seeing things in your mind's eye. This focus looks slightly out of focus or almost cross-eyed to the audience (as funny as that might sound). It is a powerful tool, especially when you get a handle on moving from one internal focus to another.

If you are in the downstage position and communicating with someone in an upstage position, you can slightly turn your head to the side that the other person is on and use an internal focus--seeing them in your mind's eye. You can then from time to time find your way (of course, directed to do so by the stage director) to an upstage position, and then look directly at your colleague.

There are few good ways to get yourself into an upstage position. You can do a sideways "V", an arch, or you can simply walk backwards (this last method can be very effective if you do it right):

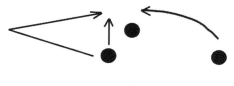

Audience

Upstage positions should always be at a specific diagonal to their partner. What this means is that, because you are in an upstage position, you have the potential of being blocked from your audience by the person in the downstage position. This is called a "sight line" problem. Here is an example of the problem:

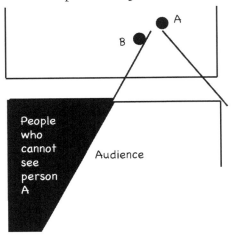

If you are moving, this is no big deal, because you won't be blocked for long. But if you are stationary, in order to fix this, you must change your angle. In the above case, simply move down just a bit until all of audience can all be seen.

Good directors are always paying attention to sight lines. You should to. If you are in an upstage position, this awareness needs to be second nature to you. Remember, singing into a blocking colleague is just as bad for your sound as singing into the wings--perhaps worse because part of the audience can't even see you.

Understand that the upstage position on stage is the most powerful one. The eyes of the audience naturally gravitate toward the person in the upstage position. This is where the negative word, "upstaging" comes from. It means you are trying to steal all of the attention on stage doing something or moving somewhere that distracts the audience from the person or thing to which they should really be paying attention.

Upstaging can sometimes be used as a comic device by a director. Someone might be singing and aria in an opera, and the director can have incongruous things happening elsewhere on stage to purposefully draw attention from the serious singing and make people laugh. This isn't always in the best interest of the person singing the aria, but it can be in the interest of the show or ensemble. During a serious section of an opera, bad directors will upstage you by having upstage business going on during your important moments. Learn how upstaging can be used productively and unproductively.

A good colleague in an opera helps the person singing on stage by subtly moving into a downstage position when appropriate. Inconsiderate singers, hoping to upstage their colleagues, and steal audience attention, stay in an upstage position while the other singer is singing a longer passage. This is not a habit to get into, and you can get a bad reputation that you don't want for doing this kind of thing. Help your counterpart out on stage by moving downstage from time to time.

Another obvious constraint in opera is the music itself. The better the composer, the more answers for dramatic interpretation are found in the score. Good music and good libretti portray feelings that are not in the words themselves. The music will create a natural period of time to move and feel between the words and the libretti will be showered with artistic sentiment and potential subtext.

In spite of these efforts by composers and librettists, meter still exists (except in some twentieth century works), notes still exist and improvisation is not really an option with the libretto. Therefore, whether straight actors like it or not, an opera singer must time his acting to these constraints. Straight actors prefer a greater degree of natural response timing to various external stimuli. The opera singer, on the other hand, must, by nature of the art form, become an expert at creating a natural response in time to the music. Again, good composers can mirror natural timing and emotional response to a certain degree. However, it is not as perfect as the straight acting alternative and singing itself elongates the speed at which people naturally speak.

Musical theater performers have been doing this for years. They must move from dialogue to songs with apparently natural and seamless acting. Singing requires elongated acting. Emotions must be spread out over the considerably slower pace of the words. It's almost like acting in slow motion. One must maintain emotions and thoughts for longer periods of time. Unfortunately, musical theater singers tend to do this better than opera singers and have really set an example as to how much one can achieve in acting while singing.

A common argument against this, however, is the fact that opera singers need to be more precise in their singing, less improvisational, and utterly even in their tone quality. These are things clearly not demanded of those who perform musical theater. So much more is spelled out for the singer in an opera score than that of a musical theater score. That being said, there is a growing argument that opera singing was never intended to be perfect singing--not to the degree of art songs. Opera singing often demands a great deal more coloring of the voice depending on the dramatic moment in the opera. The sacrifice of perfect singing is becoming more acceptable as opera again gravitates back toward is roots as a hybrid art form.

Basic Acting for Opera Singers

In order to act within the constraints of music, one must have a basic understanding of natural human behavior. When observing this behavior, you will notice a specific order that things happen. If you want to begin to look like an actor, learn this order: Thought, Movement, Words. Thoughts precede movement, and people always move before they speak. If you have dialogue to sing or speak, know that it must show in your face as a thought before you say or sing your line. If the dialogue includes something that would include a gesture like holding out your hand when you say "please give that to me," then the hand would go out before the request would be made.

You can always tell a bad actor by failing to perform with this basic order. You will often see a singer verbally express and emotion while simultaneously expressing that emotion in their face. In rehearsals, you can spot the novice when a director has told the singer to move from point A to point B on the stage. The beginner will abruptly turn their head and simultaneously walk to point B. Experienced actors will get the idea and motivation to walk in their faces first, then turn their heads and look where they plan on going, then walk to point B. This may seem like a small thing, but it makes a huge difference on stage and during an audition.

Straight actors do not like to point out the above order because they want it to happen naturally. However, when a person does act naturally, that is the order in which he or she does these things. For singers, these things need to be pointed out more often than for straight actors because, again, like it or not, feelings and emotions must be timed with the music.

Executing this natural order of events can get complicated as the music goes faster. When thoughts change quickly along with the words, you will find that the feelings and ideas that will show in your face must overlap with previous statements. In other words, while you finish saying one thing, your face will already be showing the audience that you are having the idea for the next string of words that will come out of your mouth. If you have a lot of different ideas moving rapidly, all of your motivations need to be showing in your face and changing in your face just as rapidly—only sooner.

You will notice that thinking about this could be all rather complicated. In fact, it is just about as complicated as learning the music itself. However, your goal is to find out how your character would think at this speed and in this way so that all of this happens naturally. You can try it from a natural acting point of view first, but ultimately, it will unfold in nearly the same way you see in the above example. As pointed out in the introduction of this book, sometimes learning backwards is a necessity for many who have much to overcome by way of bad habits or lack of skills.

One can learn how to act. Don't believe anyone who tells you can't learn to act. You didn't believe them when they told you that you couldn't sing, did you? Things can start out unnaturally, and become natural if you are committed to looking why these behaviors are actually natural results of true motivations.

Once you have the basic order of thoughts, behaviors, and words, you are ready to move on to some other basic ideas that will help you with your acting. The next is subtext.

Subtext

Subtext simply means that there are things that are not being said, that are *underneath* the words being sung. For example, if you are singing "Mary had a little lamb" and you just won the lottery, then you will sing the song one way. If, on the other hand, your mother just died, you will sing it another way. The words will take on the underlying feeling of the person saying the words. There is always another story going on behind your words because your character flavors those words. Your director is primarily responsible for this because he needs to see how everyone's subtext is interacting and working on the stage. A good director will know what you are supposed to be feeling and guide your interaction with others. Sometimes directors go too far in this and re-write the opera (but that's not your concern as a singer--remember, your job is to get hired back).

A good Madame Butterfly will study her part by also studying the culture of the Japanese at the place and time portrayed in the opera. She will want to understand the motivations for Butterfly's actions in the production. That understanding will add depth to her character and color everything that she does and everything that she says on stage.

When you sing on stage or at an audition, you need to be saying more than the mere words you are singing. We need to know who this person is on the inside and not just witness the behaviors. What is the personality of this character? This requires that you make artistic decisions. You should do this before you come to an audition or a rehearsal. But, be ready to have a stage director reject your concept and take you into a completely different direction. This will be a test to see if you are a team player and will do your job (let alone still remember your words--a danger if you change characterization and aren't memorized enough). You will not be penalized for selling a concept during an audition if you sell it well. But you need to be malleable to be in this business. Don't get defensive.

Good artistic directors know that there are many ways a character can be interpreted and you should too. You should also know that there are many tempi a conductor can take. There is not ultimate truth with tempi and character. There are as many different concepts as there are directors. Get used to changing on the fly.

Subtext is another foundation of good acting. What is your character really saying? What drives them? What events have just happened in their lives? How will these things affect how you sing? When Mimi sings, "vivo sola soletta" in her first act aria in *La Bohème*, is she making a pass at Rodolfo, or is she innocently telling him about her loneliness? Is she telling him she is available, or is she trying to express any fears? How she delivers the line will tell the audience a great deal about Mimi's character and personality--things that just are not spelled out in the actual words she is singing. This is subtext, and you need to think about it before you sing any arias.

Taking Your Character Seriously

In order to be convincing to an audience no matter what your character does on stage, you must be committed to believing in your character. You must believe in and be the person you are portraying. This is not easy to explain. If you are playing an idiot, don't act like an idiot--be an idiot. If you want the audience to laugh at you, you must not laugh at yourself. In other words, you must give up your self-awareness to a degree. You cannot know you are funny. You are funny because you don't realize how stupid or incongruous you are acting. If you believe in your character as a buffo baritone, for example, you must be the bumbling fool, but not let the audience know that you are aware that you are a bumbling fool. Then they will laugh.

If you want them to cry, hold back the tears and believe in the pathetic nature of your character. When you laugh at yourself, the audience won't. If you cry about your own problems, they are less likely to cry. Resisting the temptation to be self-aware is funnier and more tragic than anything else you can do. If you can come to the edge of laughter or tears and restrain yourself from going over the edge, it will be even better. The audience will demand the release and cry themselves.

If you want to be a good actor, get to know what your character would do in any given situation. You are not on stage to "mug." "Mugging" is that self-awareness we are talking about. It is not only the awareness that you are trying to be funny or tragic, but also an awareness of the audience. You must not TRY to make the audience laugh or cry. Your awareness of their existence is disconcerting to them. Trying to be funny is simply NOT funny. This is why, in theater, we have the concept of the "fourth wall." The fourth wall is the invisible one between you and your audience. Unless written in the score, or traditional like Figaro's aria in *Barber of Seville*, do not look at your audience or act in a way that you directly "play to them."

This also goes for auditions as well. It's more difficult here because you cannot hide behind a costume, makeup, and a character behind the stage lights. You are in a dress or a suit and tempted to be yourself standing before a few judges behind a table. You must not sing to them. Do not look them in the eye (even for a second to see their reactions). Your focuses (both internal and external) should be about a foot above their heads and within the forty-five degree angles spoken of earlier. If your focus is too low, your eyes will appear shut to the judges. (You can compensate for this by force opening your lids when looking down, but its easier and better just to look somewhere else for introspection). You can focus a bit higher but they don't really need to see your neck during an audition. They want to see what you are doing with your eyes and see your competency with internal and external focuses in addition to your basic thought patterns preceding your words. When you audition, put up your fourth wall.

When you are in a staging rehearsal with a stage director, put the fourth wall up between you and the director as well. Don't think for a second that you can act and then, at lightning speed, dart your eyes toward the director to see a reaction. This is called "breaking character." It really upsets directors when you do this. You cannot break the fourth wall for a second and not be noticed during a rehearsal (or a performance). The director wants to see the blocking and acting as it will appear on the stage--in its final form. A director needs to know if the concept is working, and you will ruin the continuity if you keep looking over. In addition, learn to look at the conductor with a "third eye" as well. You should never look directly at the conductor during a rehearsal or performance. You need to be completely aware of their conducting, however, but not by looking at them. Breaking character is a huge sin to a director.

Using Your Arms and Body on Stage

A separate section is needed to talk about your arms and body because it is one of the telltale signs of bad acting. For some reason, singers feel that in order to express themselves, they must use their arms and hands. There is no doubt that good actors use their arms and hands from time to time. But too many singers emulate them and bring up what is known in the business as "chicken arms." They bring their arms up in pleading gestures, constantly moving back and forth, that only distract and throw all of their energy away.

If there is reason to use your arms, some dramatic need, then by all means use them. If you are singing an aria, and continually are using your arms, you are stealing attention away from yourself. Less is always more. Instead, try to let your arms hang and then at one or two moments in the entire aria bring a hand up or reach out at an appropriate moment. This will give power to the gesture because it is not getting lost in a sea of gestures. Letting your hands hang at your side can be very disconcerting. They will feel like big monkey arms with their hands dragging on the ground. Don't worry, they are not. And don't tighten your hands into a claw, or press your hands against your sides to compensate for not being able to use your arms. Relax.

The second problem with arms is that few singers know how to get rid of their arms once they have been brought up. Many get their arms stuck. Then they try to slowly find a way to hide them and put them away, but it always feels awkward and, you better believe that it also looks awkward. Here is the trick for getting rid of arms that have been brought up for some purpose or another: let them fall of their own weight. Completely let go of them and turn off all your muscles. This will be very frightening for some. When they fall, they will almost bounce a bit of their own accord after this fast fall. Let them. It will look completely natural. You may have to practice this a few times. This is the only way you should get rid of your hands any time you use them and are done with them. Just let go of them.

As for your body, you will often think you have to move all the time too. You can fall into the same trap as you did with your arms. By moving too much just for the sake of moving, you will throw all of your energy away. Again, less is often more. Learn to stand and sing when appropriate. Do not move unless there is a reason. You need to be motivated to move. If you have no motivation except for the idea that you think you should move, don't. Your character will tell you to move.

If you have been told by a director to move at a certain point, then you must find a motivation to move. You can find one almost anywhere. You could be going to do something, think something, or get away from something. Check the score. The score will often tell you exactly when you need to move and why. Listen to the music for clues, not just the words.

Here are some more ideas that may help you improve your basic acting skills:

1. Always listen to your partners on stage. When they are singing to you, look at them and listen to them. Respond to the way they say their lines to you.

2. Look your partners in the eye. (Unless you are in a downstage position and singing yourself.) When they are singing, and it is appropriate, look at them. Where exactly do you look? Some people like looking at a point on their counterpart's nose, right between the eyes. But it is better to look into one of their eyes then the other, back and forth in rapid succession (you can't look into both of their eyes at the same time!) This will give you the look you need to show that you are really listening and also make your colleagues feel supported.

Respond to nuances of their words and subtext and feed it right back into their eyes. They will respond to it with better acting themselves.

3. Characters need to change during a show. Know that your character needs to evolve somehow as the production progresses. Who you are at the beginning of an opera should not be the same as who you are at the end. The audience should clearly see, especially through your actions and subtext, this evolution take place.

4. Know that your character is not all good or all bad. These are two-dimensional characters. Everyone is a mix. Audiences respond to your internal struggles.

5. If you are playing a heterosexual (especially guys) learn to act like one. Learn how to stand, walk, talk, lean, sit, and use your eyes like a straight guy. (By the way, this note is for all guys, gay and straight. A lot of straight guys don't know how to act straight either).

6. Please, please act when you are not singing. This always distinguishes the pros from the amateurs. The best acting you will do is both in your rests and when other business is happening on stage. The audience wants to know how you are reacting to what is happening on stage and to what other people are singing about. They will look at you for your reaction. You must not be thinking about what your next line is at that moment. If you are, you don't know your score well enough. You need to know that the person with all the power to manipulate the audience is the person not singing. If someone is singing on stage, the audience naturally turns to the others on stage for someone with whom they can relate. You see, when you are not singing, you are an "audience" to what is being sung, just like the real audience. But you are also the exemplification of how the audience is supposed to be feeling and reacting. Let the audience see your reaction in detail, and they will react the same way. They will empathize with you. This is where you can cry or laugh and make the audience cry or laugh--because you are not crying or laughing at yourself, but someone else on stage. This will give the audience permission to do the same. Never underestimate the power of your silence on stage.

7. Don't fake things on stage. Make them look real. If you are writing a letter, look like your really writing the letter, not scribbling. If

you are taking a drink, don't tip the glass rapidly--you would spill it if real liquid were in the glass (use real liquid so you get the feel)--and swallow the liquid before you sing. If you are reading a note, your eyes need to look like they are reading a note. Don't mimic behaviors; do them.

There are so many other basic stage skills we can't cover here. These are just a few of the important ones opera singers use. You will learn many more as you move along in your career. If you were not familiar with most of these before you read this book, you will find that some of them will take quite a bit of time to master. Good acting is no easier that good singing. So be patient.

As an opera singer, you are not just a singer. You are an actor, a linguist, and a musician. You also need to know how to work with many other kinds of artists including designers (set, costume, and lighting), librettists, and choreographers. Finally, you will need to learn to work with administrators and businesspeople. You will need to learn to be a businessperson yourself. This is so important that it takes up the entire second half of this book. Hang in there. This is all learnable. Take your time and learn each skill well. Too many singers are in a hurry for some reason. Don't be. There will always be jobs. Study hard, don't skip skills and steps and learn to do things well. There are many singers out there who were in a hurry and didn't learn their skills thoroughly enough. But there is a lot of room at the top of the opera business, just not in the middle. So master your career from the bottom up and don't take shortcuts.

Section Two

The Business

Chapter 10

The Truth about Education

H ere is the truth many schools do not want you to know: they are there to serve you and your goals. You are not there to serve their goals. What is the point of a diploma or a piece of paper telling you that you have completed an established curriculum? Who cares if you jumped through hoop after hoop set up by others who may have different goals than the ones that you have? If you want to become an opera singer, understand that no opera company will ever ask you for your transcripts or diplomas. They don't even want the information on your resume.

Most institutions of higher learning are set up to serve themselves. They bestow degrees that lead the continuation of the institution. These degrees are mostly important if you want to become a teacher. In the real world, degrees are irrelevant.

Does that mean that education is equally irrelevant? Absolutely not. The only reason anyone would ask that question is because school systems have successfully convinced people that a degree in their institution should be equated with an education. You need to understand that those that live the professional lifestyle are not the same people that create the curriculum of educational institutions.

Education is absolutely necessary to a successful career in opera. The best question a potential opera singer can ask is "Where can I learn what I need to know to become a successful opera singer?" Can you learn some of these things at a university? Sure you can. Can you get important information out of a conservatory? You bet. Does the piece of paper matter? No.

This is so important to understand because the temptation will come after a student enters a university or college to finish the offered degree. However, all too often this will mean that you will spend more money, and jump through many unnecessary hoops before you can get started with your career. Be patient with the things you need to learn, but don't waste time on the things you don't. If you are not sure that you will be an opera singer, you might as well go to a university and complete your degree until you know. If you are not sure, you won't be doing what it takes anyway to be a successful opera singer. The only people who should be professional musicians are people who know in their hearts that music is their calling. Career opera singers never got to the top by just fooling around with their time or by splitting their focus among various talents. They certainly didn't get there by creating something to "fall back upon."

Many singers in the field of opera have enough university credits to have a doctorate, but don't even have a bachelor's degree! Why? Because they understand that school is a tool. A university is there to serve you in your goals. If you can stay focused on your goals, then you can learn quite a bit at the right institution of higher learning. However, erudition is tempting, and learning for learning's sake is a seduction. It's easy to stay in the cozy, comfortable cocoon of college.

However, if you want to succeed in opera, you need to eventually stop going to college and start doing. You will discover that although some education will be necessary, you will learn more by doing than by going to school. You will also learn more quickly. The apprentice model of the past would be the best way for someone to prepare for a career.

So, let's assume you are entering an institution and aren't going for the degree, but are going for the skills. What do you need to know that is taught in most schools in order to become a professional musician? What course work is generally a waste time for those seeking a career? Below are a couple of lists to answer these questions. Of course, in the first list, left off are the things included in this book, generally not taught in these institutions.

Worthwhile classes:

1. <u>How to sing.</u> This is number one ahead of all considerations. Your time in the practice room is sacred. It is better than getting good grades in ANYTHING else. It's what will get you jobs. Your job is to sing like a god. It is neither to be pleasing nor simply good. You must practice daily, sacrificing all else--even grades. All vocal habits are created through a daily lifestyle. You cannot cram vocal technique. In addition, it will take you the most time to master--more than any other skill you gain in any other class. (See the chapter on teachers to read about finding the right teacher).

2. <u>Piano.</u> Most of the successful opera singers in big houses play the piano as well as sing. Piano skills make you a musician and not just a singer. You cannot be good enough on this instrument. At the very least you should learn to accompany yourself on arias and ultimately you should learn to work your way through an opera score with enough piano skills so as not to need a coach or accompanist to teach you the notes of the opera. Piano skills make you more desirable by opera companies as well because they know they are hiring a real musician.

3. <u>Music Theory.</u> Every musician needs this. You abilities to interpret and opera score and understand the intentions of a composer are enhanced with this knowledge. You need to understand the nuts and bolts of music and harmony if you want to even pretend to understand what you are doing as an opera singer. You need to be more than a trained monkey.

4. <u>Ear Training.</u> Along with theory, the development of your ear is absolutely necessary. You need to be able to read music, both melodically and rhythmically. Professional conductors do not have time to waste (in big opera houses especially) waiting for you to adapt to changes, interpolations, new or assigned ornamentation and stylistic changes in interpretation.

5. <u>Music History.</u> You aren't a musician unless you understand where you came from. You need to understand how music evolved and how that evolution affected what you are singing. As a professional opera singer, you are expected to be an ambassador for the art form. If someone asks you a question about the composer you are singing and you can't answer, how can you represent this art form? You can't. You need to understand why we have music and understand the philosophy of its existence as well. This knowledge will make you a better performer.

6. <u>Conducting.</u> If you can't conduct at least a little bit yourself, you can't follow a conductor. You will be working with conductors your entire life. One of the most frequent complaints of conductors is about singers who can't follow them and go off on their own merry musical way, expecting the conductor to follow them at all times. Again, your first job as a singer is to get hired back. Study conducting and get the basics of an ictus, a prep gesture, and other techniques that will help you communicate properly with conductors.

7. <u>Diction and Language.</u> You will spend most of your life performing in foreign languages. You cannot act in a language if you don't know every word you are saying--and that is EVERY word. As stated before, a director will ask you in front of everyone present at a rehearsal what a specific word means. The director may do this if you look like you don't know what you are saying. Learn your operatic languages fluently. As for diction, your job is to sound like a native. All diction classes will teach you to write all your languages phonetically with IPA symbols. This skill will save you scads of time. Professional opera companies often have a diction expert behind a table taking notes on your pronunciation.

8. <u>Opera Literature.</u> Many schools actually don't offer this, and others don't make it a requirement. This is a must for aspiring opera

singers. You need to know which operas are being performed in the world and the titles of the most famous arias. In addition, a good class will teach you to recognize famous voices--not just of the past, but of the present. In addition to knowing the operas written by the most prominent composers, you need to know the ones that will correspond to your voice type--the ones that will be your bread and butter operas. There will be operas you will specialize in and sing again and again.

9. Performance Practice. Unfortunately, this in generally only offered during a Master's Degree. You need this. There can be a huge difference between what is written on a page and what you actually sing. Composers had their own set of rules about how they expected their music to be interpreted. As previously mentioned, music publishers still produce Mozart opera scores that confuse ornamentation signs with fermatas. Sixteenth notes in Puccini are not always evenly performed and Verdi's dotted rhythms are often intended to be performed as double dotted. How would you know this unless you did your homework? There are many things that composers expected that you just would know and it wouldn't have to be explained. Nowhere is this worse than in recitative that is incorrectly executed and interpreted. Not only is it unfortunate that students are made to wait until they do graduate work to study this topic, but also that most of these universities have no performance practice classes geared specifically toward opera and opera singers. This is a huge need in schools.

10. Performing opportunities. A singer needs as much time on stage as possible. Institutions that serve opera singers need to offer as many performance opportunities as possible. They should do multiple opera productions a year, and include oratorio and concert work. Unfortunately, most schools weight their performances in favor of choral music. If this is the case, go to another school.

11. Acting classes. (See the chapter on acting). Unfortunately, these classes at most schools are not geared toward acting and stagecraft for opera. Even most conservatories do not offer this, but ought to. Study what you can in this area.

Classes you may want to avoid:

1. <u>Solfeggio (you know, Do, re, mi).</u> Many will consider this sacrilege to attack this practice but this can waste more time in college than many things. If one wants to play the piano, for example, you will succeed if you see a note on a page and read it directly to the note on the piano. How ridiculous would it be to have to add the intermediate step of having to name the letter name of each note before you play it--especially after years of having done it! If you are learning a foreign language, you speak best by thinking in the language, not by translating it into English in your mind first before speaking each word. Solfeggio is such a practice. Instead of having students practice sight-reading directly, schools make you associate a syllable with each note, significantly slowing down the process of reading music for many. Many schools require years of classes teaching this practice and considering the cost of tuition and credits these days, this is highway robbery.

2. <u>Composition, Orchestration.</u> These classes are great for composition majors, but too many schools are requiring this of regular music majors. Theory is enough, unless you plan on honing those writing skills.

3. <u>Choir singing.</u> We've spoken quite enough about this in this book (especially in the chapter on Legato technique). Choir singing can be a menace to classical singers and should be in a different discipline. Manipulation of the voice is necessary to blend, getting rid of the natural vibrato and portamento. No opera major should be required to sing in a choir.

4. <u>Some Twentieth Century Theory.</u> Understanding theory as it relates to your craft is certainly important. There are many twentieth century operas out there and an appreciation of twentieth century music is important. But classes requiring you to analyze and not simply understand many practices like twelve tone rows are an utter waste of time. You will not be required to ever analyze a twelve-tone row in your life as an opera singer. Similar twentieth century practices

are equally interesting but time consuming and simply will not be used in your profession. Understanding the history is one thing, but jumping into the advanced theory is quite another. There is a point to which your time is being stolen from you.

5. Art Song Literature. Singing it is fine; studying it isn't necessary. Although singing art song recitals is wonderful, no one gets paid to do it much anymore. You can study this in your own free time for enjoyment. It doesn't further an opera career. Schools spend ninety-five percent of the time teaching you art songs, so as not to harm your voice. This is fine, and there is much wonderful literature out there. However, if you are not going right back into teaching, it's not necessary to study the literature for a career.

6. Experimental Music classes. Many schools indulge professors by allowing them to waste your money and time with required classes in philosophy, musicianship integration, and others often rehashing skills that you have already learned or don't need as an opera singer. Watch out for classes shoved into the curriculum that serves a particular professor and not the student.

7. Advanced Form and Analysis. Like some twentieth century theory, understanding form and analysis on a basic level can be important to becoming a well-rounded musician. The question arises as to how far one needs to take this information to serve their particular discipline. This is certainly another piece of how music is put together. Understanding the nuts and bolts of a da capo aria is very useful. But most schools go overboard in requiring far too much of this. Admittedly, it is hard for schools to cater to the professional goals of all their students. This is the problem with established curriculums and diplomas in general. These courses of study are there to serve a generalized population (many of which are there to become teachers themselves) and not to serve those entering specific musical professions. It's hard for them to do this. This is why you can use a school to get information, but shouldn't feel compelled to complete its established curricula.

8. Bibliography techniques. A completely scholarly class designed to teach you to do research. This has nothing to do with

anything you will ever use as a professional opera singer. Stay away unless you plan on becoming a scholar.

9. <u>Dissertations and papers.</u> Same as above. You are not studying to be a writer. You certainly need to know how to read and find information about opera in a library, but again schools can go too far in your needed skills. If you plan on writing, then do it. If you plan on teaching, do it. Doctors love to write papers that only other doctors can read and understand. They keep all their education inside their educational bubble and all too often have little connection with the outside world or those who are actually doing the things they are writing about.

10. <u>General Education.</u> You won't find this much in a conservatory. However, there is an argument to be made that you should know basic information about the world and about being a human being. Understanding science, history, government, economics, writing, English, psychology, and math are important parts of being human. However, schools can go overboard and also require things you don't need or already know. The best suggestion is to test out and challenge classes that don't fit your goals or about which you already possess enough knowledge. Understanding basic life information can serve you in your life, but may not be necessary to your present goals. Be careful when just blindly following any set curriculum at a university.

Final words on Education

Education should continue throughout your life. If you stop learning or stop working on your voice, your career will stop as well. You should be an expert at what you do and constantly be making yourself more valuable. That being said, all too often the attitude of those at educational institutions is that your chances of becoming an opera singer are so small that you will have to end up becoming a teacher like them. Far too many teachers are frustrated performers. Unfortunately, many of them were seduced by the educational system themselves, which drew their attention away from the things that could have ensured a career for them as well.

Do not get sucked into the plans or goals of an institution. Spend the majority of your time singing and honing your craft. That's what will count if you want to make a living wage at opera singing. Schools are a useful and even a necessary tool in the path to your profession. But don't ever lose sight that it is only tool to help you along your path and not an end in itself.

If you are not committed to being an opera singer, then this information may not be for you. Instead, you may desire to spend the thirty thousand dollars or so a year to "find yourself." But that's an expensive bill that you (or your parents) will be paying for years to come. The expense of educational training these days has gotten so out of hand that it is almost worth it instead to find yourself a private tutor or expert in the field and study all of your skills privately than participate in an institution. Do the math and do what serves you best. You will spend your time in life either working for your own dreams or working for those of others. Try to make the right choices along the way.

Chapter 11

The Truth about Agents

D on't even think about getting an agent until you feel you have your technique is at a level that audiences wouldn't flinch to see you perform at a major opera house. In addition to that technique, in today's world, you need to be an actor too. Competition is immense; agents know this and are not going to waste their time with you if you don't have your act completely together. This means that when you open your mouth, you know what it going to come out. There is no room for hoping or wondering what the quality of your performance will be like.

Now, before you go looking for an agent, you need to know what agents do and what they represent. They do not represent you as a person. In fact, get it into your brain right now that they will not have any of your personal interests at heart. You are a piece of meat to them and many of them will tell you that in just those words if you provoke them or whine about why they are not caring about your life goals. This is nothing but business to them. If you can make them money, then they will be interested in you. If you are looking for a friend who wants you to grow and improve, then you are not ready for an agent.

Do agents sell you? Actually, not very well because it is too dangerous for them. This is an important aspect to agents that you must understand. Remember the character of Larry Tate on the old television show, *Bewitched*? The man was a chameleon, ready to change his opinion to match that of his client at a moment's notice. This is the way an agent works.

Let's make this even clearer. An agent cannot sell you as well as you will sell yourself. Each agent represents many singers. Now put yourself in his or her place for just a moment. Let's say that you are selling a tenor to San Francisco Opera. If you sell that singer strongly, telling the company how wonderful he is, how they can count on him, and how the audience will love him and then the opera company has a bad experience with that tenor, what will happen? Your reputation as an agent will be ruined. You may ruin your ability to sell other singers to that company. Therefore, you cannot afford, as an agent, to ever truly take a hard stand on any singer you represent.

As a singer, you will be lucky to have your agent say to a potential opera company, "I have a singer that might interest you." That's about as strong as it can get in order to protect the agent's reputation. If you really want to be sold, you will have to hire a marketing manager. This will cost you. Many singers have made their careers by having big money machines behind them with huge marketing campaigns. For example, a marketing agency will take a huge amount of money and approach Columbia Records, for example. They will pitch a recording with say, Placido Domingo or Renee Fleming. Then, they will put you on the recording with them. This is fame by association. They can hardly turn down the offer because they are footing the entire bill for the recording including the fees of the famous artists. In essence, they have bought your fame. If you can get a machine like this behind you, you have it made (you do, of course, have to sing well). They can make sure your picture is in *Opera News* every month.

Agents don't do this dirty work in general. Most of the jobs you will get, especially in the beginning, you will get yourself, through word of mouth and networking. When you do, the agent will take a percentage. Then why get one?

There are a number of reasons to have an agent. Agents make opera companies feel more comfortable. Companies don't want to have a negative relationship with the singer before they even hire them. They prefer to avoid conflict regarding contract negotiation, and also don't really want to have to tell a singer to their face that they don't like their voice and why. An agent provides a company a layer of protection. In addition, many companies expect that an agent will act as a screener to weed out bad singers and thus not waste an opera company's time during an audition process.

As you see, agents serve mostly opera companies before they serve you. How do they serve you? They can set up auditions to which you might not have access. They can negotiate higher amounts in your fees (they want to do this because it serves them). They will send out letters, resumes and demo tapes for you. They are often more connected than you will be at the beginning of your career.

Many singers try to live without an agent. Some actually succeed. Even some singers who are singing in bigger opera houses don't have agents. Some singers are extremely personable and terrific networkers. Some singers, after having done their homework, have the guts to call the big companies themselves and say the right things at the right times and get jobs.

But for most others, they need to play the agent game. So, how do you get one?

How to Get an Agent

Once you have decided to get an agent, you need to get him or her to listen to you. This is not an easy task, especially if you are a soprano. Sorry, Sopranos, but you will need to be ten times as good as any man to get noticed. The sad thing is that not only are there many more sopranos than men that want to become opera singers, but there are far too many sopranos that think they are better than they are. There is a lot of room at the top, but for sopranos, it is especially true that there is not much in the middle.

Most singers stop at this middle point. They are good and getting noticed. They get paid for small gigs, and Grandma brags about them. There is an endless supply of singers that fall into this category. However, if you want to make a living as an opera singer, you have to be better than good. Your goal needs to be shock and awe. If you don't force an agent's jaw to drop in astonishment with what you do, you will have to settle for being lucky to succeed.

All singers have their bags of tricks unique to them. You need to know what you can do that almost no one else can. What is your specialty? Does your repertoire reflect that specialty? When you get an agent to listen to you for the first time, you will have limited amount of time to sell your product. Sing what you sing best. Make sure you are over your stage fright.

So, how do you set up that first appointment? Singers do this in many different ways. Here are some suggestions:

1. Start by doing your homework on agencies. Get a copy *Musical America*--borrow one or go to the library. *Musical America* lists all the agencies, singers, and opera companies and other artists in the field. Read the rosters of each agency. See whom they represent. Some agencies represent big names, some medium, and some take on the has-beens. Be careful whom you sing for.

2. Put together a packet about yourself and send it to your list of agents. The packet should include a cover letter (well-written in GOOD, captivating English), a prose bio, a resume, and a headshot. If you want to go the extra mile, include reviews and photos on stage. In your cover letter, mention that you will be on an "audition tour" in New York City (or where ever the agent's office is located), and would like to set up a time to have them hear you. Tell them you understand that their time is limited and will meet them at any time convenient to them--even during their lunch, for which you offer to pay. Let them know that it will be worth their time to hear you. Make sure this is true! If you are not ready and blow the audition, word gets around

and you will hurt future chances of being heard.

3. Follow up your packet with a phone call (or two or three). Tell them you will be glad to pay for a rehearsal space (there are many in NYC) with a piano--remind them about paying for their lunch. Tell them why you chose them as an agency. Be charismatic. Tell them you will be worth their time.

4. Many will turn you down. If they do, there are other ways to get them to listen to you. There are many ways to think on your feet. Network. Ask coaches which auditions are in town. Sometimes you can even crash an audition and get an agent and an opera company to hear you at the same time. Remember, you better know that the only thing keeping you from greatness is to get someone to listen to you. If you are wrong about this, you may blow your chances of ever being heard again. If you sing fabulously, they will forgive anything, because that is what they are looking for--wonderful singers. So make sure you knock their socks off. However, beware of stalking. Sometimes singers don't have any finesse in getting people to listen to them. They hound agents and opera companies with phone calls, emails and sudden appearances out of nowhere. You don't want to get that reputation either. You can hurt yourself. Most times you will have one chance for them to hear you. Even if it has been two years and your technique has improved, they won't want to hear you again because you didn't have enough sense not to sing for them the first time--so they don't trust you. Luckily, there are a lot of agents and opera companies out there, and if you blow it, you don't have to ruin your career.

5. You need to stay aware of the needs of the agency. Most agencies have a roster of singers that represent all voice types or fachs. If you are a spinto tenor and they already have three spinto tenors that they represent, you are competing against the agent's own roster. They won't be interested. Agents love specialization. You may hate the fach system and the classification of voice types. You may be able to sing both Rossini and Verdi. However, when agents sell you, they prefer to classify you. They may make you choose between two things you do well. They can more easily sell you this way. They don't want to defend you or get into uncomfortable conversations with opera

companies as to why you can do both Don Ramiro and Siegfried. Agents are always asking themselves where you are the most marketable. They don't ask what you want to sing or what makes you happy (at least until you are a superstar--raking in the money for the agency).

Singing is a Business

Agents have many different kinds of contracts. Most agents charge ten percent for operas and fifteen percent for concert and oratorio work. You pay them whether you got the job or they did. You usually reimburse the agent for postage and phone calls. They will often send you a monthly bill. Every once in a while, an agent will try to charge you a monthly fee to represent you. This happens especially with sopranos (they feel they are doing you a favor, if you are a soprano). Stay away from these agents. If they don't believe in you enough to take you on without a fee, then they will not do you any good in the opera world. These are not serious agents. If you are wonderful, good agents will want you because you will make them money.

Don't try to become their friend. Be cordial and be businesslike. Too many singers do not understand the business mind. When you sing at an opera company, your primary goal is not to sing well or create a beautiful artistic product. It is to get hired back. Like any business, an opera company, like agents, is there to make money first, art second. If you are lucky, you can do both. But if you lose sight of this truth, you will get into trouble.

Singers who don't understand this will often get into debates with agents, stage directors, conductors or even other singers about artistic considerations. This is death to your career. If a horrible stage director tells you to sing directly upstage, you shut up and do it. If a conductor tells you to breath or phrase in a way that would cause the composer to roll over in his grave, you say, "You bet!" If they smell that you don't like them, you will not only not get hired back, but other companies will not hire you as well because directors, conductors, managers, agents and other singers all talk. Get this straight into your head and do your job.

At a recent panel discussion of General Directors at a Classical Singer Convention one afternoon, a room was full of singers eager to ask questions. One singer asked the question, "Why don't we sing all of our operas in English?" Many of the General Directors tried to answer this question. One CEO after another tried to explain how it could affect their "bottom line" or how many donors as a percentage preferred opera in the original language, or how difficult it would be to negotiate with singers contractually who had to learn an opera in more than one language or with multiple translations. The faces of the singers in the audience were blank and many were scratching their heads. They seemed at an impasse until one General Director, who had been a performer, offered an artistic answer, explaining why the music is better in using the libretto that first inspired the composer to write the music. Suddenly, heads were bobbing, and smiles crept upon everyone's face. They weren't interested at all in issues of development, accounting, or contracts. They didn't want to understand why a union orchestra will walk out of the room five measures before they are done playing a sitzprobe of Madama Butterfly.

There is a huge disconnect between artists and businessmen. So here is your bottom line: If you want to succeed in this business, you better understand the business side, no matter how painful, unartistic, and boring. You need to understand what drives your opera company and your agents. They don't need nor want emotional outbursts or long treatises on your life dreams.

Are they all this inhuman? No, some try to walk the tight rope. But when the cards are down, and they have to choose, they will choose the business. They have to if they want to survive. Agents are the protectors of this system, and they protect the opera companies in the same way. If you learn to treat your singing not only as an art, but a business, you'll be able to create a solid career that can last as long as your voice does.

Chapter 12

The Truth about Auditions

There are a lot of truths about auditions that you may not want to hear. For one, they don't get you a lot of jobs. For another, opera companies often hold them for reasons other than actually looking for someone to hire. Many times, they have already decided upon someone to hire. The truth is that it is extremely hard for any opera company to determine how good you are in five minutes. They can't tell if you will be easy to work with or if you have the stamina to last through a three-hour opera. Opera companies would rather call another opera company, a director, a conductor or other friend and ask for a recommendation.

Word of mouth is the primary way by which serious auditions occur or by which singers get hired. A serious audition is an audition that is not a "cattle-call" audition, but one that has been set up because someone recommended you. Some companies won't even require this much. If the recommendation comes from the right person, they may not need to hear you at all, or they may simply ask for a recording.

Unfortunately, most of the auditions agents will get you will be of the "cattle-call" variety. You will pay your accompanist, not to mention your travel and parking expenses each time you do these auditions. After hundreds of these, you can rack up quite a bill. Of course, you will get your name and voice out there for people to hear.

But getting your voice out there isn't enough. It's important to know that if they like your voice at an audition, they will probably need a recommendation of some sort before they hire you at any of the larger opera houses. This is because larger opera houses don't like to take chances. They can't afford it. Too much money is spent on production and development. Because they don't take chances, the very biggest houses have prompter's boxes and multiple covers for principal roles. So don't expect that an audition alone will get you the big jobs. You must have a reputation to accompany that fabulous audition.

This means that when it is time to audition, you better know what you are doing. Too many students come out of school without any training in audition techniques. In addition, they know very little about what opera companies are looking for during an audition.

The Basics of Auditioning

The first thing you better do when you audition is to know the opera for which you are auditioning. If you have a good agent, he or she will tell you. If not, make sure you find out yourself what needs to be cast. If it is a specific opera, please sing something from that opera if possible. A company doing *Elixir of Love*, for example, would prefer to sit all day and hear "Una furtiva lagrima" than hear anything else from another opera. You may think that this would be horribly boring for the company, but you are doing them a favor. They need to compare voices, not repertoire. In addition, if you sing something obscure, they will be listening to the song and not to you. Your voice needs to be memorable--not your song. If you don't have a song ready from the opera the company is doing, you may have a strike against you, but that doesn't mean you shouldn't audition. Instead, sing what you sing best--but again, do something that most people know.

If you are going to a cattle-call audition set up by your agent, you will find that agents generally have a time slot given for all of their singers to audition. You could stay at one of these auditions all day and hear one singer after another who sings all of the notes, words, and rhythms perfectly. If you think that you will get a job by default by not missing any of those three things, think again. Music is not about notes, rhythms and words. It is what you do with those things that is the beginning of creating music. An opera company is looking for so much more than robotic reproduction of a score.

How do you phrase and interpret your music?

Are you easy to work with and can you take direction?

Can you act?

Will you look good on my stage?

Will your voice blend with the soprano that I have already hired?

Each company has its own set of criteria it is looking for. Your job is to do as much homework as you can before you get there and then be prepared to give the company exactly what it wants.

Here are some of the basics of doing the audition:

1. The entrance. When you enter an audition, try not to turn your back or your backside to the judges. This is most obvious when you give your music to your accompanist. Don't give it to them from the front of the piano. Walk to the back of the piano (upstage side) and hand the music to the accompanist. Walk confidently.

2. The introduction. Introduce yourself in a clear voice, loud enough for all to hear and understand. Speak with confidence and speak with the voice that will tell the judges that you are charismatic, easy to work with, and friendly. You may be judged before you sing a note by the way you introduce yourself. In most auditions, they will ask you what you are going to start with. If they have time for a second aria, they will pick it from your list and tell you.

3. <u>Beginning your aria.</u> In opera, as opposed to musical theater, you traditionally do not nod to your accompanist to begin. You begin with your gaze down and when you are ready, you raise your head and create your first focus. That will cue the accompanist to begin. When the accompanist begins the introduction, you must be in character. The music of the introduction must reflect the thoughts of the character you are representing and those thoughts must reflect in your face. Your acting begins on the first note of the piano, NOT the first note of your singing. When you begin to sing, you shouldn't suddenly move any part of your body--not even your eyeballs. Smoothly let your acting glide from the introduction to the singing. Why is acting in the introduction so important? Because if you don't do this, you will send a message that you only act when you are singing, and that you will be disconnected to your character when you are not singing on stage. If you don't understand the importance of this, you need more acting classes. True actors are revealed in the rests and not in the notes.

4. <u>The singing.</u> Nail the high notes. This will anger some singers, but there is a reason they are called the "money notes." Remember, opera companies are a business. Know that most artistic administrators will decide to hire you in the first ten seconds or less. They will know if you understand phrasing and legato, whether you circumnavigate your register breaks correctly, whether your vibrato is annoying or your tone beautiful, and if you look like you understand every word you are saying in the language of the aria. It doesn't take long to make this judgment. After this decision is made, the rest of the aria is there to see if you can maintain this positive vision that you set up in those beginning seconds. Finally, you better end the aria with style and skill. They will remember the last thing you sing more than anything else (except a missed high note).

5. <u>The acting.</u> Today, it is not enough to be a good singer. You have a few minutes to show that you are comfortable with your body, that you feel at ease moving around, that you understand your words, and that you look as if you are improvising the whole affair. If you don't understand that thoughts precede physical actions, which in turn, precede the words you are singing, then you don't understand

basic acting and should take some classes or work with an acting coach. Audiences of today no longer can countenance "park and bark" singing. Opera is a dual art form that purposefully combines acting and singing. Don't be fooled into thinking this isn't necessary. If your educational institution preparing you for an operatic career were doing its job, it would require much more in the way of acting training. (See the chapter on acting).

6. <u>Your dress.</u> When you audition, without wearing an actual costume, wear something that will help the opera company see you as the character for which you are hoping to be hired. For example, a red dress might aid a potential Carmen, a pants suit could assist a Cherubino or Nicklaus, or an unkempt tenor without a tie, hands in pockets, might help a Nemorino. However, if unkempt, make sure it's on purpose. If you don't know, classy and semi-formal are generally safe.

7. <u>What to bring.</u> Bring your resume and a headshot. Make sure your headshot has your name on it. You would be surprised as to how often pictures get separated from resumes and get lost in the shuffle. Some singers staple their pictures to their resumes.

8. <u>The Accompanist.</u> Find out before you come if you need to bring your own. Most times you do. If not, find out if you have to pay for the provided accompanist. If you use the company accompanist, you can't depend on how well he or she will play. So don't complain. If you complain to the company, you do so at your own peril because the accompanist is probably a friend of the company. However, most accompanists can be controlled if you, as a singer, know what you are doing. Tempi can be controlled, for example, if you are expert in making sure the vowels are guiding those tempi and not the consonants. Consonants not preceding the beats give the impression to your accompanist that you are slowing down. Unfortunately, again, too many singers come out of school without being taught anything except how to complain about how their accompanist didn't follow them.

9. <u>What you look like.</u> Many of you are not going to want to hear this, but you must. Especially in today's television and movie society, your looks make a huge difference in getting hired. Get over

this now. Only at the MET are there exceptions to this rule. Everywhere else, you need to look the part as well. If you are overweight, it doesn't matter if you are a Fiordiligi, but don't expect people to take you seriously as someone dying of consumption, as Violetta or Mimi. If you want to sing those roles today, you will be competing against women who not only sing fabulously like you, but also look like Teresa Stratas did when she did those roles. (You may not need to be that thin, but you can't look chunky). Companies are even getting tired of the audience tittering when Cio-Cio San tells everyone they she is only fifteen years old. Today, you need to sell yourself, not just your voice to get certain roles. It helps to know what the company is looking for as well. Sometimes the director is looking for something very specific to fit a concept. Because of this, you shouldn't take it personally if you look fabulous and sing wonderfully, but are still passed over.

How to Write a Resume

Another thing left out of school training is how to write a resume. It's amazing how many different kinds of resumes are sent to opera companies. Most of them end up in the circular file. Why? First, far too many are unsolicited. But those that are solicited often reach that circular file as well because they are unprofessional. Here are some basic guidelines to writing a professional resume.

1. Keep it to one page. Companies don't have time to waste reading page after page of information. Take the best stuff and dump the rest. Get to the point. If you do keep to one page, please use a font size everyone can read. Don't make it smaller so as to fit more information. Put a one inch margin around all the edges. You want the resume to look clean and simple.

2. Make sure the resume fits the audition. Don't hand a musical theater resume to an opera company. Make sure the primary focus of your audition is at the top of the page. Keep information off that doesn't build support to being hired by the opera company.

3. Opera Section. List your operas by composer on the left column. Then to the right, put the name of the role, then to the right of that, put the year you performed the role. Don't feel the need to list where you performed the operas (you may not want to if it was only in college) unless you sang it at a major opera house. If they want to know where you performed a particular opera, they will ask. If you do not have enough operas to put in this section, or are just starting out, call the section "Opera Repertoire" and instead of the date, put the words "in rep." Now an important note on this subject: don't put the opera down as "in rep" if you haven't coached and learned the opera. If you haven't been hired, hire yourself. If you are out of work and aren't motivated enough to study operas on your own time without a contract, then you may be in the wrong business.

4. Concert Section. If you don't have enough operas on your resume, you can add concert work. This section isn't really necessary if you are auditioning for an opera. If, however, you have sung with any major symphonies or choral organizations of note, you might include this.

5. Awards Section. You can include competitions you've won and other honors.

6. Coaches and Master Classes. Include master classes and coachings with well-known people in the business. This is optional.

7. Languages and Other Information Section. List languages you have studied. After each language, you can put your degree of fluency (like fluent, good, passable, conversational, etc...). You can include special skills here, like piano proficiency (a huge plus in the opera world. It tells everyone you are a real musician), movement and acting experience, juggling, fencing training, etc...Sometimes this is a good place to put something very interesting about yourself that will make you stand out from among your colleagues.

8. Education. This will be sad news to some of you, but your degrees and diplomas don't matter. Your agents will strip your degrees from your bio. They will also strip any mention of coaches and teachers that are not famous. So take them off your resume.

Most companies don't even care about your resume (unless it looks awful and have no operatic experience, then it will stand out against you). Most of your education and experience does not matter as much as your exceptional singing. If you sing poorly and your resume says you have a doctorate from Juilliard, it won't matter at all. In fact, it will hurt Juilliard and not help you. No one will ever ask where you studied as a question to determine whether or not to hire you. That is why it is left off bios. Experience is more important. What have you done and what are you prepared to do? But even job experience pales next to a voice that doesn't work properly.

What can you put on a resume if you are mailing it to someone to make it stand out? Nothing. Your cover letter will be most important. And then, the first sentence should read "Mr. Such and Such (an acquaintance of the person to whom you are writing) referred me to you" or "…wanted me to contact you." That will get their attention--referrals. If you really want to be remembered by someone, meet that person. Find a way or place to shake hands (please--no stalking folks!). If you get this chance, make your introduction short, sweet, and memorable so that when you send follow up materials or ask for an audition, you are already fresh in his or her mind.

Now, assume that you give a stellar audition and have a nice, clean, impressive resume. You will not be alone. Some people have this down to a science and Artistic Directors know this. Some people are professional auditioners, and when you put them on the stage, they have no idea what they are doing. If you have the opposite problem (many do not audition well, but do perform well), you need to learn how to audition and treat it like a performance. Get over the judgmental nature of the audition and any desperate need to be hired. People can smell your loathing and desperation a mile away.

So, once you have your act together, what do you do? It often comes down to personality. Do they want to work with you? Are you a phony or are you a genuinely nice person? Is your manner a pasted on technique (as if you've read *How to Win Friends and Influence People* one too many times), or are you authentically easy to work with? Most companies these days would rather take an inferior voice with a great personality, than a superior instrument that is connected to a self-obsessed diva.

Final Words about Auditioning

In the United States, opera is mostly a flavor-of-the-month affair. This means that singers are constantly auditioning, even after they are singing in larger houses. You will be in one house for a month of your life, then in another opera house. Each one will require an audition. This is much different than any other job in the U.S. where you get an interview for a job, get the job, move to a city, and keep the job for many years. The idea of a resident company where you can stay indefinitely is just not an American phenomenon. You can have this in Europe, however. You can audition once and stay for a while. This is a fabulous situation, if you don't mind living in Europe. If you plan to sing in North America, however, you better learn how to audition for a while. The light at the end of the tunnel can be seen eventually when you have enough companies hiring you back again and again without auditions or your network and word-of-mouth opportunities are such as to sustain a living income. It can be done with enough patience and perseverance. Don't give up, and don't stop practicing.

Chapter 13

How to Build Experience

B efore an agent will look your way, you need to have some experience. You can't put out a resume that lists the arias and art songs you know. You need stage time, and lots of it right away.

There are two reasons you will sing for an opera company--one is money, the other is experience. In the beginning, you probably will not do it for money, so get over that right now. Assuming your voice is beautiful, and you have the stamina and projection necessary, and your teacher and coaches agree that it is time for you to begin, you need stage time any way you can get it. You need experience working with directors, conductors and other singers.

Before you can sign with an agent, you should have roughly ten or more leading operatic roles on your resume. Your singing is actually more important, but there is only so much for which your voice can compensate. If you have no stage experience or very little, you won't be trusted.

The best way to become a great performer is to get on stage

again and again. You can study all day, but there is nothing that can take the place of performance opportunities. In the beginning, you will find yourself in those situations where companies will not want to hire you because you have no or little experience and leave you wondering how you are supposed to get that experience.

First, you should consider living in a metropolitan area, like New York City, San Francisco, Houston or Chicago. Around these metro areas, there are many small opera companies that need good singers that they don't have to pay--or at least pay much. If they won't hire you for a lead, start with small roles to show those that run these small companies what you can do with your voice. But make sure you have a lead voice (and are not deluding yourself). If you do, they will eventually use you in a lead. Be sure to ask them for what you want and ask them what you would have to do in order to get a lead role. Ask them to be honest if they are reticent about giving you the opportunity. Ask them where you need to improve.

Can you move from chorus up the ranks? In some small companies, you can (not in the big ones). But you need to be up front about it. Tell them you are willing to sing chorus for them, but would like them to consider you for small roles and lead roles eventually. If they say you are not good enough to get small roles right away, you probably haven't studied enough. Small companies do not usually have the funds to pay for comprimarios, and so they pull them from the chorus. Always be frank and ask them to be frank as well about your skills and what you need to be considered. If you are not planning on a full time career and you are a professional opera hobbyist, don't bother asking to do lead roles. Companies need committed singers, hungry to build their repertoire.

If you have prepared your voice properly, small companies will want you as a lead. Understand that while you may have been the top dog in your school, but you will not be in the real world. Your degree, even a doctorate, does not mean you sing well enough for companies to want to hire you to do their leads. You need outside opinions. Find yourself some small opera companies and get started. You can look in *Musical America* or on its website for a listing of opera companies nationwide. Even most of the small ones are listed.

There are many interesting small opera companies around. In New York, for example, Amato Opera, with a tiny little stage and house seating only one hundred seven patrons, will perform an opera eleven times, with eleven different casts! No real work with a director, but you get a video with the staging and a dress rehearsal. Best of all, it goes on your resume.

Other small companies have great artistic reputations in spite of their low budgets. As such, in a metro area, they will often attract singers from the local big opera houses who want to attempt a new role out without trying it out on the big stage first. This can be a coup for you if you get a job with one of these companies in that you can have an opportunity to work on stage with seasoned professionals. You want this and you want to become friends with people who are doing what you want to do.

Small opera companies love singers who don't complain about money. They are usually struggling to make ends meet themselves. They usually have a volunteer staff. So treat them well. When you get your first job at a company, there are some rules you need to keep:

1. <u>Do not gossip.</u> Don't talk negatively behind the backs of singers, conductors, or directors, to other singers, conductors, or directors. It will be hard to avoid this because so many do it. It always gets back to them. Always. And then it hurts your career. Other singers will regularly try to suck you into negative discussions about others. Don't participate. This is when you have to learn to walk a tightrope. You don't want to make an enemy of other singers, so you may not easily walk away from uncomfortable conversations if it will offend them. However, you also don't want to be participating in those conversations. Sometimes, you can steer a conversation to something more positive.

2. <u>Always be early to rehearsals.</u> Be there at least fifteen minutes before start time. Some companies will put this in your contract. It is frustrating to a company when a singer not ready to go on time. It is disrespectful, and it costs the company money. People are being paid, like the accompanist, conductor, director, and union orchestra to be there at a specific time. Some companies will fire you for this. By the

way, don't get lost on your way to your first rehearsal. If you can't find your way to rehearsal, you will immediately have a strike against you--they will think that if you are directionally impaired in life, you will also be directionally impaired on stage.

3. Always be completely prepared with your music. That means you are not holding your book. When you arrive at a company to rehearse, you know your music cold--but not only cold. As stated earlier, you need to know it so well that when the stage director gives you blocking or a character change that you didn't expect, you don't suddenly forget your music. It means you must over-memorize. Be ready for anything.

4. Always be completely prepared with your blocking. This means if you have previously been blocked into a scene, the next time you get together to go over the same scene, you have the blocking down cold. Community theater is about rehearsing at a rehearsal. Opera is not. You are expected to have rehearsed and completed work on your staging before repeating a rehearsal on the same page numbers. The director fully expects to work on nuances of acting at the second rehearsal of the same pages--not reiterate blocking that was already given to you. If you don't know your blocking, you may be fired. Don't go to bed after a rehearsal unless you know that every step of blocking and instruction from the director has been meticulously written down in your score. No matter how smart you think you are, if you do not write it down, you will forget the blocking.

5. Never talk back to a director or conductor. You can get clarification, but don't them read an iota of disdain in your face about anything they have asked you to do (you can however, discuss some things--for example, if you are not comfortable performing naked or some such thing). But, keep artistic disagreements to yourself. And, this isn't just in a public rehearsal, but generally also in private. They are your bosses. Their job is to create the artistic vision for the show. If the director asks you to sing upstage or stand on your head, (and he probably will at some point in your career), do it without complaint.

6. Learn to be part of an ensemble. The show is not about you, even if you are singing the title role. Don't be a diva. Ever. The show is better when the group works together with a common goal.

7. <u>Respect the chorus.</u> The chorus is usually local and foundational to an opera company. When you leave, they will still be there. What they think of you plays a huge role in whether the company hires you back or not. Remember, that is your first goal--to get hired back. Don't act or believe that you are better than the chorus. You couldn't be doing what you are doing without them.

8. <u>Respect the technical assistants, costume designers, makeup artists, set builders and other professionals involved with the production.</u> Even though they are not in the spotlight, as you are, don't believe that they aren't as valuable as you are. You are part of their team. It's better for you to think you work for them than they work for you.

9. <u>Never discuss money or your contract with anyone else in the company.</u> This is death. Know now that everyone is not paid the same. Some have been hired before and get more money. Some are harder to replace and make more money. If you are one that makes more and reveal what you are paid to another singer, that other singer may go the General Manager of the company and complain. You will probably not be rehired. (And neither will that singer). This is another reason many opera companies prefer to work through agents. If you are not working through an agent and representing yourself, you must be doubly careful that they still like you by the end of your run. Companies are businesses, and do not like singers to kiss and tell regarding contracts.

10. <u>Never back out of a contract.</u> This is death to your career. If you are working for a smaller company and suddenly a larger company comes your way and makes you an offer, it is the height of unprofessional behavior to take the better job. If you do, you will get a reputation for not being trusted. Other, even larger companies will know that you might throw them aside for something even better. Contracts are everything in this business. Companies need to count on you. They advertise you and promote you. If you want a career, your first thought is always about supporting the company and not yourself. If you look at companies as your enemy or adversary, they will be able to tell, and you will not get hired back. The trick to getting

hired back (always your first goal), and about dealing with most businesses in the world, is to tell them what you can do for them-- NOT what they can do for you. Be a team player always.

11. <u>Don't double book.</u> Some companies have this in their contracts. Having rehearsals that overlap with another organization or company can create all kinds of problems. Emergencies arise and rehearsal schedules get changed and that can create conflicts. Rehearsal schedules are one of the most difficult things for a company to create. If the company is a small company, they might ask you for conflicts ahead of time. Then they will try to see that everyone in a particular scene can be in the room at the same time for staging and musical rehearsals. The complexities of doing this are beyond the patience of most companies. Larger companies wouldn't dream of asking for your conflicts. They will give you the rehearsal schedule, and you will have to adjust. By the time you get to larger houses like New York City Opera or San Francisco Opera, you will often find out your schedule for the next day the night before. Do not make plans you cannot change during a rehearsal period. Nothing can give a company more headaches than this. Make this as easy on the company as possible and you will be loved.

12. <u>Be someone everyone wants to work with.</u> No matter how introverted you are, don't separate yourself from everyone. This is a networking business. Be friendly and professional. Be positive and helpful. Try not to upstage your colleagues. Take notes when the director and conductor speak. Make sure they can see you are taking notes. Make sure they know that you want to get their vision down on paper--that it means something to you. They will love you for this. Look for ways to be kind to people and make their experience better. Try not to think in terms of what it is doing for you and your career. It will do a great deal for your career if you care for others beside yourself. And don't think any opera company is too small to make a difference in your career. Remember, everybody talks--up and down the ladder from small company to large. Singers, directors, and conductor also move up and down the ladder performing at all size companies. Your reputation is money in your pocket.

13. <u>Don't whine or ask the company for special favors.</u> Don't

ask for extra comp tickets and don't ask to come late to a rehearsal. Don't tell them how hard your life is and want them to cry with you. This is a business, not therapy. Everyone's life is hard, and everyone makes sacrifices to make an opera happen. Respect others by not whining about your problems.

14. <u>Do not surprise anyone during the performance.</u> Do the blocking you were staged to do during the rehearsal, whether you agree with it or not. Wear the costume you agreed to wear. Take the tempi you agreed to take. If you change your performance from what you did in rehearsals, you can say goodbye to being rehired again.

15. <u>Follow up on getting pictures and reviews of the performance afterward.</u> This will help your publicity and the company will be happy to send them as long as they liked you and want to have you back.

16. <u>Never bad mouth the company after you have worked there--even if they deserve it.</u> Word gets around. It will get back to them one way or another, even from people you are sure you can trust. Message Boards are read by companies and other singers. There are always two sides to a story and if you bad mouth a company, someone will come and ask for their side of the story and the company will bad mouth your reputation right back. Whether you are right or not, you do not want to be in this situation.

17. <u>Send a thank you note after the performances for giving you an opportunity to perform.</u> You cannot believe the impact this small token of appreciation will have.

18. <u>After the performances, send the directors you worked with at the company an email and ask them for an honest assessment of your performance.</u> Ask them what they think you could do to improve. Listen carefully. They will tell you not necessarily what you may consider the truth, but they will tell you what is important to them and what they felt they didn't get out of your performance. Don't write back and argue with them. Write them and say thank you.

19. <u>Keep in touch with them with updated activities and ask them if there is anything for them in the coming season.</u> Now this is important: if they have nothing or offer you nothing after you ask, it is

because, painful as this may be to you, that they didn't like your performance enough to hire you back. It will be easier for them to look elsewhere than hope you will give them what they want. This is especially true in a larger company that has singers waiting in line to perform there. If this happens, don't accuse them of these things or of not liking you. Instead, after a number of months or a year, write them back telling them that you have done a lot of work on your technique (and your acting) and would like to audition for them again, so they can see the change. If you do audition again, make it count. If they still don't hire you back, it's usually because they didn't see the change or because you didn't spend the year improving yourself. You should always be improving yourself and also be markedly better to a company from year to year.

Final Warnings and Advice

Building experience takes time and patience. Your voice also needs time to mature. Because you will not be making a lot of money during your growing period, you need to find work that gives you control over your time when a job suddenly comes your way. You don't want to lose your job because you suddenly have to be gone a month. Teaching privately can be a good way to do this, depending on how much wear and tear it takes on your voice (especially if you are a teacher who talks a lot). Getting a job in music is best, if you can get it. However, stay away from jobs that will tempt you or suck you into a steady paycheck and cause you to abandon your dreams. Be careful of the "golden handcuffs."

A word of warning about building your skills and experience: Be wary of vocal programs costing ridiculous amounts of money. There are singing vultures out there with programs in other countries that promise all kinds of things. Ask yourself, "Can I get this same training by paying directly for it for a lot less money?" For example, if you are in New York already, you are surrounded by talented acting and vocal coaches, diction experts, language classes, conductors and other professionals who can coach you privately for a lot less than these so-called programs. You should know by now that most of your biggest breakthroughs that you have achieved have been by yourself in your own practice room. Teachers and coaches can guide, but there are some things that you must do alone and figure out by yourself. Programs are no substitute for plain hard work on your own. When you participate in a program, you are not only supporting the paychecks of their teachers and coaches, you are supporting the corporation or business that offers the program. This means you are paying administrative costs and additional markups.

While you are building your resume, if you want to do competitions, do them. They are not necessary. If you win, you can get performance opportunities or money. That's the best part. If it is only "prestige," don't waste your time. They can also be good for getting you up on stage in front of people--and that's good too. Just know that, although you may put it on your resume, it won't matter a lick during an audition. Get what you can out of the competition. If opera companies are there and hear you nail your performance, then great. However, mass exposure can have a drawback. If you don't nail the audition, all those companies will remember your failure. For this reason, although it costs a bit more to pay an accompanist for multiple auditions, it is sometimes worth doing rather than risking failure at a competition in front of so many.

When you are not working, coach and learn operas on your own. Study your languages. Improve your piano skills. Don't waste time. You can build a basic resume quickly after college if you keep improving yourself and are willing to work for free. Do it and don't complain. You are building your future.

Chapter 14

Teachers, Coaches, and Accompanists

N othing is more important to you as a future opera singer than making the right choices regarding how you will learn how to sing. Learning to sing can be a complicated affair. You will learn most in your practice room. Outside that room, you will learn from books, teachers, coaches, conductors, and even other singers. The smart singer will listen to advice and information from many sources. Then that singer will adopt what works and throw away what doesn't work. This can be a difficult process, because singers often do not know whom to trust. There is competing and contradictory information everywhere.

In order to survive this confusion, you need to begin by knowing the difference between a teacher, a coach, and an accompanist. You need to know the difference between legitimate pedagogy and national preferences and opinions.

Finding the Right Teacher

Don't think for a minute that because someone has a "Dr." in front of his or her name that it means that person knows anything about singing. First, it's important to understand what the "Dr." means. It means the person did graduate work. One of the principal differences between the Bachelor's degree and graduate work is the idea that you are given rules during undergraduate work and you are debating rules when you do graduate work. The goal of most graduate studies is not to answer questions, but rather to ask more questions. By the time you get to become a doctor, you will be skilled at debating the truth of just about anything in your field, and simultaneously being able to footnote it and add astonishing bibliographies.

In other words, once you are a doctor, you have a wonderful ability to disagree with other doctors. Education doesn't always bring you closer to the truth. That is not the goal of educational systems. This problem is compounded by the fact that once you receive your doctorate, you can more easily get a job at a university than those who have been successful singing on the world's stages. A person who has thirty years experience in the professional world has very little chance against those who have the piece of paper and have achieved nothing professionally. Those who oversee department accreditation, themselves doctors, support this flawed system by penalizing departments who don't fill a quota of hired doctors. Nothing offers a more scathing commentary about the university system than that. If universities did their job, they would hire people who have done it-- who have had a successful singing career for a minimum number of years. Working in the private sector should be the requirement of every serious school of music in the world. Unfortunately, they often cannot attract these professionals because they don't pay enough.

So, how do you choose a teacher? Here are some guidelines:

1. <u>Stay away from teachers who think they own you, or who belittle you.</u> The vocal world is full of teachers who are full of

themselves. The goal of a great teacher is to get you to a point where you can fix yourself and don't need a teacher anymore. Find someone straightforward, but kind.

2. <u>Find a teacher who tells you the truth about your voice.</u> You are not paying a teacher to compliment you. Too many teachers are afraid of telling you that you have certain vocal problems because they think you will begin to manipulate your voice. For example, if you have a fast vibrato, they should tell you. Anything that will keep you from a career is something you want to know. You don't want a mean teacher, but you want a teacher who is not afraid to tell you the way it is.

3. <u>Find a teacher who has been a successfully paid performer.</u> It is even better if your teacher made a complete living for a while from professional singing. Stay away from students who went right into teaching. Many think they know what it takes to be a professional and do not.

4. <u>Find a teacher who knows how to communicate.</u> Many professionals can sing superbly, but have no idea how to tell a student what they are doing. Teaching is a separate skill, just like performing. You need a teacher who has both things going for him or her.

5. <u>Find a teacher that teaches the vocal techniques explained in the first half of this book.</u> If your teacher denies the existence of register breaks or the in-between notes required for legato technique, run away as fast as you can. Also, if he or she doesn't teach coloratura technique, find someone who does and who understands that it is a technique for all voices and not just lighter or higher voices.

6. <u>Find a teacher who understands the Italian school of vocal technique</u> and is aware of how it differs from the English, French and German schools. Find a teacher who gives more than lip service to bel-canto technique.

7. <u>If you are a man, study with a man.</u> There are few exceptions to this because most women simply do not understand the upper registers of the male voice and how they sing exclusively in their chest voices. If men study with women, they often come out with falsetto-like high notes or a "mixed" upper register. Women do not train by extending their chest voices into the stratosphere like men do. Even if

they can explain it, they cannot demonstrate. Demonstration can significantly cut down on your learning time.

8. <u>Find a teacher who is not afraid that you get input from other places.</u> There are no perfect teachers who know everything. If your teacher doesn't readily admit this, find another one. This book doesn't provide all the answers either. Your vocal technique will ultimately be a mixture of ideas from many different sources that you have adopted and that work for you. No one teacher or coach can or will give you everything you need. However, you will have one person that can be at the center of your basic technique building. This is important, in part, because every teacher has a different vocabulary that you need to learn. You don't have time to keep learning everyone's vocabulary, but rather you need to get on with the business of learning to sing.

9. <u>Find a teacher who plays the piano.</u> Not only will you save money on accompanists, but you will have someone who can adapt quickly during a lesson and quickly guide you through problems from the piano. It will also mean that your teacher will be a well-rounded musician, which is what you will need to be if you desire a serious performing career.

10. <u>Find a teacher who loves music and loves the voice.</u> You would think that could go unspoken, but there are too many skilled musicians in the world who no longer enjoy what they are doing. It is just a job, and there is no love or passion in music anymore. They no longer cry at beauty, but see music as a technical exercise and a weekly paycheck. Make sure your teacher still has that glimmer of excitement in the eyes when discussing music.

11. <u>Find a teacher who doesn't try to "steal" you away from other teachers.</u> As you begin to improve and people notice your abilities, teachers, coaches, and others will suddenly start soliciting you and asking you to work with them. Understand that your success will add to their reputation and that that is why they are trying to flatter you and seduce you into studying with them. Be careful and differentiate between these kinds of people and those few who legitimately have your best interests at heart.

Finding a Great Coach

Most singers, practicing a consistent few hours a day, and studying with the right teacher, won't need a teacher any more after about eight years. They will be at a point that they are self-correcting. What this means is that they don't need to be told HOW to fix their voices, but rather only need to be told what is wrong with the sound and are able to fix their own voices instantly.

Coaches begin to take the place of teachers as the student progresses. They should be differentiated from accompanists, who are paid less. Here are some things to look for in a good coach:

1. Good coaches will be master pianists and accompanists. They will be able to play anything and especially be familiar with the operatic repertory. If they are paying too much attention to their playing, they won't be able to listen to you and give good feedback. So make sure they are beyond competent on the keyboard.

2. Good coaches will be linguistic experts. One of their main jobs is to make sure that you sound like a native. They are experts at diction. Depending on your repertoire, they need expertise in Italian, German and French. Some coaches have additional specialties in Czech, Russian, Portuguese and Spanish, if needed. Too many coaches are weak in the area of English diction. They feel that if you both speak English, you don't need it. Nothing can be further from the truth. Your goal is to be understood from the stage, and English diction is a weakness not only among singers in other parts of the world, but among American singers as well.

3. Good coaches will never tell you "how" to sing. That is the job of a teacher, not a coach. The coach's job is to tell you what they hear and let you fix it by yourself or with your teacher. Too many coaches cross this line. Stay away from them. Many think that they have heard enough lessons and read enough books to make them understand enough about the voice to teach. Let's be absolutely clear

here: If you haven't done it and learned to sing beautifully yourself, you cannot tell someone else how to do it and shouldn't try.

4. <u>Good coaches know performance practice.</u> You need a coach who knows the style differences between Verdi, Puccini, Mozart, Donizetti, Rossini, and Bizet. You need a coach who understands the rules of ornamentation of each composer and can demonstrate how to do a correct recitative. You need a coach who understands the traditions of opera as well.

5. <u>A good coach can sing other people's parts</u> that are singing against you and still play the accompaniment. You need to feel how you fit into an opera while rehearsing and know what the other parts are doing. Good coaches give you the full experience.

6. <u>A good coach understands the libretto and poetry of song.</u> Being able to tell you what the score is trying to say is important in your interpretation. The coach needs to understand the motivation of words and how they affect the music.

Finding a Super Accompanist

A pianist is not necessarily an accompanist. Far too many singers and pianists themselves do not know the difference. Some of the most fabulous solo concert pianists cannot accompany at all. Don't be fooled by their excellent solo technique. All too often they will begin to play, believing they are playing just another solo and you end up feeling that you are there to accompany them. Here are some things to look for when seeking for an accompanist:

1. <u>They are not coaches or teachers.</u> Accompanists do not get paid as much. Like coaches, they do not tell you how to fix your voice, but neither do they tell you any of the things a coach will tell you. They don't fix your diction, or tell you what seems to be wrong with your singing.

2. <u>They are followers.</u> They know how to sit on the edge of their seats and wait for subtle signals telling them how to respond to and match every nuance of your expression. A great accompanist is

almost psychic in their ability to anticipate your phrasing and spontaneous emotional interpolations.

3. They understand the different styles of different composers and periods. Although they try not to talk about your singing as a coach would, they need to know the same things as a coach would regarding performance practice. Their playing needs to reflect the intentions of the composer.

4. They need to be inspirational. Their playing should be completely expressive and motivate you to sing. You should not be spending brain time trying to pull your accompanist along with your expression. Neither should you have to spell out to your accompanist how to execute a phrase. Instead, your accompanist should fill you with the joy of singing.

5. They prepare as if they were being judged themselves. Too many accompanists feel that they don't need to hit all the notes because they are not the ones under scrutiny. They are wrong. Missed notes make the singer look bad. A singer shouldn't have to worry about whether the accompanist is drawing attention to himself through bad technique. A good accompanist knows that his or her job reflects on you whether you are singing in a recital or doing an audition.

Final Words on Specialists

Working with the right people is foundational to your success as a singer. Outside of these right people, you need to keep your ears open to ideas from other singers, directors, conductors, and even fans. Do you have to accept all of their advice? Not at all. You just need to listen to people who may have important information. Everyone will not have useful information. But you need to read books, coach with people in the business, and interview people who are doing what you want to do. Then you, intelligently, need to keep the stuff that works and throw out the stuff that doesn't. Everyone at the top has climbed a different ladder to get there, and you will learn to sing in your own way and develop your own vocabulary that makes sense to you.

Don't be afraid to try things out. If you are smart, you don't have to cave in to the fear-mongers. If Placido Domingo hadn't ignored everyone who told him he would ruin his voice by singing Otello, we wouldn't have had his amazing contribution to the role. Sing with your voice and you won't need to worry about ruining your voice with different kinds of repertoire. If it works, using your natural voice, keep singing. If you have to push to try to sound like others who have sung the repertoire, then don't sing it. You can be smart and don't need to constantly be protected by the proponents of the "fach" system.

Surround yourself with positive people who will support your dreams and goals. You should be the slave to no one. If you are not sure that those giving you advice are working for you, get more advice from elsewhere. Experiment intelligently. If you do, you will achieve everything you want in your career.

Chapter 15

Lifestyle and Money

C an you make a living as a singer? Of course. The sad thing is that far too many people in the United States have this notion that people can't make a living in the music field. Too many schools support this negative view of the profession. Universities all too often encourage you to get your degree in music education, get certified to teach, or have a second major that you can "fall back on" when you abysmally fail at opera singing. Of course, when you create something to fall back on, you generally do. Put out that safety net, and you will drop.

There are so many ways to make a living in music, a comfortable living. First, decide what lifestyle you want to have. Second, decide how much money you want to make. You have to decide for yourself what is important to you in your life. Finding balance is different for many people. This is another area that is sorely lacking in schools. They can teach you all about music, but then they abandon you when it comes to managing your singing business. Since these two things are vitally important to your success, they warrant a closer look.

Lifestyle

Deciding on your lifestyle must come before money. Money can be made in different ways, depending on how you have chosen to live your life. Some people want to raise children and others prefer to marry their profession. Either way, you will need to understand the demands that will be made on your life.

If you stay in the United States, you will be traveling a great deal. Each U.S. opera house will hire your as a private contractor for a period of usually three to six weeks. Then you will go to the next city and the next opera house. The more you work, the more money you make. The more money you make, the more you will be away from home. This is tough on American singers who also want to raise families or be part of a local community. Of those, some make enough to bring their families on the road with them and homeschool their children. Others may end up not seeing their children very often. In fact, for this last group, the distance from family can get rather trying, and many singers will stop singing to raise their kids. Many others, more than you know, have attempted long distance relationships that only end up in painful breakups.

I know this isn't glamorous and the purpose of explaining this isn't to discourage you from having a singing career. Many try to make this work. One alternative for some singers wanting to stay stateside and still raise a family is to try to mix their opera career with oratorio and concert singing. Some agencies will work with this and emphasize their concert work and others will not. Be sure you have an agent that will allow you to do this before you sign your contract with them. Actually, concert singing generally pays better than opera for less work and less time. There is very little rehearsal compared to opera. It's such a good deal for the singers that agents usually take fifteen percent instead of the ten percent that they take for opera.

Another alternative for the singer who also wants a family life is to go to Europe and get a "fest" contract. You can become the house lyric tenor or the house dramatic soprano in a single opera house and come home at night to your family after rehearsal. You might be separated from extended family, however. But if you don't mind living in another country, this may be your option.

There are many singers without attachments who marry the profession. In this position, they actually have much more time to hone skills, and constantly perform. Agents love these types because they are singularly focused and bring in a lot of money. There is nothing to divide their focus.

If you are a singer who wants a family, you need to know that you will be competing against those who don't. They have more time, more focus, and more of an ability to jump when their agents or opera companies tell them to jump. Don't think this means that you should give up if you want a family. In fact, there are arguments that actually favor you.

For one, there is the argument that relationships can center you as a human being. This can make you easier to work with because you have learned to be less self-centered. There is also the argument that one purpose of art is to help people become better human beings. If so, how can someone who has never lived the life of a normal human being (without community or relationships) show the world a better way? Can you separate the art from the artist? Certainly, these are philosophical ideas. But they are worth mentioning to those who might be discouraged because they want a career and a family. You might have trouble competing in some ways, but you may also have the capability to be a better artist.

Everyone is different and everyone wants different things. You will need to adapt your career to the lifestyle you wish to live. You should be thinking about this before you start making decisions that leave you in no-win situations like those that leave you backstage crying before a performance because you haven't seen your kids for three months. Create a plan. Decide before you start, what kind of life you would like to be living, and what would be happening in every area of your life if things were working out the way you would like. Then create a plan to get there. It will be different for each person.

When you design a plan such as this, you should get out a piece of paper and write down each area of the perfect life you would like to live--in detail. This means write down how often you would be willing to be gone singing, how many hours a day you would like to spend with your spouse or children, how long you would set aside for practice, how much time for self-improvement and staying in good physical shape. Always start with the end in mind when setting goals, then move toward the place you are right now, so you can create a number of possible paths to get there.

Designing a lifestyle is not an easy task. You will see quickly that you can't do everything. Balance is always required for peace. Designing your life is a necessity if you want to achieve it. Don't just let life happen to you and then find yourself in a situation you don't want.

Money

So, now that you've decided how much money you need, you have to design a way to get there. In general, as a singer, you will live a bit differently than most people do when it comes to money. You won't have a steady paycheck. Your monthly income will vary. You will be self-employed for the most part. Your money will come from many different sources. Things can get rather complicated.

There are financial advantages and disadvantages to your lifestyle. Budgeting will be more difficult. Verifying income when buying a home will be more difficult (you may need limited documentation or stated income loans). However, you will have tax advantages, you will have free travel opportunities, and because you are an artist, people will help you and give you things. In addition, you will always have some income because the chances of all of your income sources simultaneously firing you are next to nothing. For this reason, being a musician is more secure financially than having many of the so-called "real jobs" out there in the world.

Because you will be self-employed, you need to know how to

run your business. You need to read books that teach you about managing money. Artists in general do not like to do this. Their minds are generally messy along with their houses--very "right-brained." However, in order to be successful in singing, you need technique, in spite of the fact that you wish it was all expression. Also, in order to be successful in a singing career, you need to know how to crunch numbers, budget, and do basic bookkeeping and accounting. Listen carefully: if you are not in control of your money, you cannot maintain a career in music. So, like it or not, you need to spend time learning a few skills that seem to have nothing to do with music. Here are some skills that will help you along the way:

1. <u>Learn to reconcile your bank statement.</u> Get a computer program like Quicken or QuickBooks and use it daily.

2. <u>Learn to budget your money.</u> Understand completely your income and expenses. Plan. Stick to your budget like a fiend.

3. <u>Learn to save.</u> You will have summers and winters in your career. When you are making more than you need, save, save, save for the times you have months that you are not making money. Also, learn to invest. Understand compound interest and how it can work for you.

4. <u>Get out of debt.</u> All debt. Debt is a killer, especially for artists. If you have student loans or credit card debt, pay them off NOW. Every penny you think you have isn't really yours if you have debt. You cannot maintain power to keep your career alive for long once the stranglehold of debt grabs you. Don't get into debt either-- except maybe for a home and maybe a car. If you can, don't go into debt for those either. If creditors are calling, it will affect your career and your singing. Learn to differentiate between your needs and wants. Have only two cards with a ZERO balance: American Express and a Visa. The Visa is for emergencies and the Amex has to be paid off every month. Establishing credit is important for things like a home purchase, but debt should be avoided.

5. <u>Learn about the insurance dollar.</u> The insurance dollar is the ratio of what you pay in insurance premiums verses the chances that the bad thing will happen that you are being insured against. The problem is that insurance is often a huge scam charging thousands of

percent in fees to put in the pockets of corporate fat cats. To avoid these scams, you need to understand the different kinds of insurance you buy--including life insurance, health insurance, and car insurance. Prices vary greatly, so you must shop around. Understand the laws where you live and what is required of you regarding insurance. Creating your own insurance savings accounts can often be more reasonable. Understanding and reading about getting insurance can and will add more to your lifetime wealth than most anything. Too many singers make huge mistakes in this area sucked in by fear of catastrophe.

6. <u>Understand taxes.</u> As one who is self-employed, you need to keep meticulous track of all of your expenses. You will be surprised as to how just about everything but food has the potential for being deducted from your taxes. Since you are a performer, how you dress, how you cut your hair, what make-up you use, what music you buy, books you read can all be attributed to business expenses. Do your research and read books about getting the most out of your deductions. Find a tax person friendly to the arts is also important. Besides insurance, your understanding of taxes is the next thing that will contribute the most or be the most detrimental to your lifetime wealth.

7. <u>Constantly make yourself more valuable.</u> This doesn't only apply to opera, but to other parts of your life. Add skills to your arsenal that can be marketed. Keep improving teaching and piano skills. Learn operas when you don't have to. Improve your language skills. Take a directing or conducting job.

8. <u>Learn how to market yourself.</u> Don't think your agent will do everything for you. They won't. Learn to network. Hang out with singers, conductors and directors. Hobnob with wealthy donors. Get your name out there. Learn how to approach people that even your agent is afraid to contact. Remember that your agent will never sell you like you will.

9. <u>Get hired again.</u> Your first job is not to create your art, but to get hired again. If you get too obsessed with creating great art, you may have difficulty getting along with directors and conductors who don't know what they are doing. Then you get blacklisted. You will

create great art from time to time, but if you start arguing and talking back to others in power over you or even other singers, you can hurt your business. Then you create NO art. Isn't that worse? Learn to get hired back. Most of your life work will be done by going back again and again to the same places because they love you. This also makes your life easier and reduces auditioning.

10. <u>Don't limit your sources of income.</u> Opera may be your main focus, but you can do oratorio and concert work, give recitals, teach master classes, teach private students, teach classes, work in recording studios, direct or conduct shows, or do weddings, church services and funerals. These are all ways in the beginning that you can make ends meet while you build your career and resume.

Too many singers do not know anything about business. They often do not realize that singing is a business and not only an art (at least for those that live in capitalistic societies). Most schools do not have the time or resources to require any classes on maintaining a business based on musical skills. If you want to have a career as a singer, you must learn about money on your own, like it or not. Once you have set your lifestyle goals and done your homework about money, you will have a foundation in which you can create more art and support all of those years of voice lessons.

Chapter 16

Final Sentimental Words

This book wasn't intended to scare anyone, but it may separate those who thought music would be an easy major in school from those who understand that studying music can be just as hard as becoming a lawyer or a doctor. It's generally not as lucrative. But that's not why you do it, is it?

The fine arts are a necessity of life. They build non-discursive thought and fashion foundations to creative thinking that, in turn, produce those who design solutions to the world's problems. Opera does this best because it is a synthesis of all the art forms. Certainly some prefer their arts in separate doses and that's fine. But opera has the capacity to do so much more than any of them alone. Be proud to have an interest and a motivation to study opera. We don't have enough of these kinds of artists in the United States.

School children in Europe run to wait in lines at the opera houses after school, so that they can see an opera in standing room that evening. Arts play a central part in Europe's identity. Because the arts are emphasized in their schools, they are stronger in most subjects than American children. These European school kids know our history and literature better than we know theirs. They speak more languages than we do. Studies show that students who study the arts in school, especially music, test fifteen points higher on IQ tests than those who do not.

Music creates synaptic connections between the hemispheres of the brain, the abstract and the concrete, the random and the sequential. Don't let anyone tell you that the arts are not a necessary part of our society or tell you to "get a real job." You are told this by people who are ruled by fear. Nothing is more real than delving into the nuts and bolts of humanity and the subtleties of its expression than through studying the arts.

When you study music, you learn more than a song. You learn more than how to sing that song. You learn about patterns of humanity. You learn about weakness and frailty, power and strength. When you perform, you learn about giving free gifts and about the negative power of hopelessness and fear. As an artist, you transmit these things to others and make society grow, prosper, and understand more about itself.

The more you study and tear apart the music, the more you tear your own soul apart. When you put the music back together, you make a new creature not only of yourself, but also of those who hear you sing. You cannot separate the art from the artist. You also cannot separate the artist from the society of which that artist is a part. Teach the world to put aside fear. If the explanations or ideas in this book are useful to you, then use them to stretch yourself, split yourself, refine yourself, and renew yourself. Be an instrument in the hands of society to build bridges to hope and peace.

These words may be a bit sentimental to some of you. Please understand that we don't learn information for the sake of learning information. This book was not written to make one person feel superior to another or to satisfy the intellectual voyeur. It was written to help you build skills that will increase your ability to express your unique self, to inspire society and to change people for the better.

There can be meaningful power in information if it is used to serve others.

If you keep your focus on the reasons you are studying this information, you will develop the patience necessary to obtain all of the skills you desire. They will not come overnight. They will come in time. There is no hurry. Remember that you are not living for the performance, but for the path that leads there. Your time rehearsing and improving should be the most precious part of your life. That's where you will learn who you really are and become someone that will help others come to know themselves as well. Peace in your journey.

For more information on the author, including upcoming engagements and his other publications, visit danmontez.com or wholenotepublishing.com